1,001 FACTS

ABOUT THE PROPHET
JOSEPH SMITH

ALSO BY

ALEXA EREKSON

Disney Till You're Dizzy:
1,001 Facts, Rumors, and Myths
about Walt Disney World

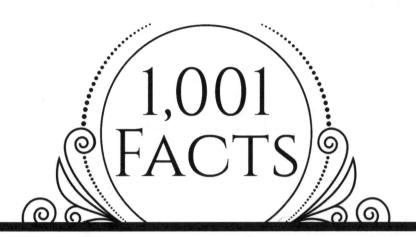

1,001 FACTS

ABOUT THE PROPHET
JOSEPH SMITH

ALEXA EREKSON

CFI
An imprint of Cedar Fort, Inc.
Springville, Utah

ISBN 13: 978-1-4621-2199-1

Published by CFI, an imprint of Cedar Fort, Inc.
2373 W. 700 S., Springville, UT 84663
Distributed by Cedar Fort, Inc., www.cedarfort.com

LIBRARY OF CONGRESS CATALOGING-IN-PUBLICATION DATA

Names: Erekson, Alexa, 1996- author.
Title: 1001 facts about the prophet Joseph Smith / Alexa Erekson.
Other titles: One thousand one facts about the prophet Joseph Smith
Description: Springville, Utah : CFI, an imprint of Cedar Fort, Inc., [2018]
  | Includes bibliographical references and index.
Identifiers: LCCN 2018004030 (print) | LCCN 2018007070 (ebook) | ISBN
  9781462128945 (epub, pdf, mobi) | ISBN 9781462121991 (perfect bound : alk.
  paper)
Subjects: LCSH: Smith, Joseph, Jr., 1805-1844--Miscellanea.
Classification: LCC BX8695.S6 (ebook) | LCC BX8695.S6 E74 2018 (print) | DDC
  289.3092--dc23
LC record available at https://lccn.loc.gov/2018004030

Cover design by Jeff Harvey
Cover design © 2018 Cedar Fort, Inc.
Edited by Erica Myers and Nicole Terry
Typeset by Kaitlin Barwick

Printed in the United States of America

10 9 8 7 6 5 4 3 2 1

Printed on acid-free paper

To Ashley, Kennedy, and Brooklyn. As the three women who were there during the best two weeks of my life, you guys will always have a special place in my heart. I would not be here without the experiences and memories we shared on the Church History Trip 2014.

(And, as always, to my husband, Dalyn.)

CONTENTS

INTRODUCTION

I HAVE HAD A DEEP EMOTIONAL CONNECTION TO THE PROPHET JOSEPH SMITH ever since I was a little girl. The first time I read about his martyrdom, when I was eight years old, I bawled my eyes out! Whenever we spoke about him in church or seminary, I felt exceptionally interested and invested. My two favorite scriptures of all time are about him. The first time I visited places like the Sacred Grove, his home, the Kirtland Temple, Nauvoo, and other Church history locations saved both my life and my testimony. I was diagnosed with idiopathic gastroparesis at twenty years old; it was devastating. My dreams of graduating from college and becoming a registered nurse were shattered. Then I found a new passion: writing fact books. My first book is called *Disney Till You're Dizzy: 1,001 Facts, Rumors, and Myths about the Disneyland Resort*. Only a short while after it was published, the Lord told me that it was time to write a new fact book. This time, Heavenly Father wanted me to write a fact book for Him, about the Prophet Joseph Smith. I was nervous and shocked. I was accustomed to writing theme park books. I never thought I would have to write about something so serious, important, and even controversial. But I knew that if God commanded me to do it, He would help me through it. I was right. God helped me every step of the way.

I have been in Sunday School, seminary, and institute classes when the teacher has said something along the lines of, "We are probably past the point of being able to discern fact from fiction regarding some aspects of Church history." While there might be some truth to that statement, I still disagree. With the new project of the Joseph Smith Papers, several biographies, and the knowledge and studies of Church historians and scholars, there has never been a more perfect time to determine the real facts behind the life of Joseph Smith. At the same time, with social media, the internet, and an epidemic of fake news, it has also never been easier to spread lies and myths about the life of Joseph Smith. There has always been confusion and falsehoods regarding Joseph Smith's life, even since he was a mere fourteen-year-old boy.

As I was studying for this book, I stumbled upon an internet article from a bitter former member of the Church. The article tried to use certain elements of Joseph Smith's life to ruin the testimonies of others. I read through the entire argument. As somebody who has studied the life of the Prophet intensely, I knew and understood the full story from the original sources before I read this article, which provided only misleading or twisted information. This person wrote about specific things in Church history without including the full story or explanation. I could see how using this—and other articles like it—as the main source of gaining information can easily mislead those who once believed in or are trying to learn about the truth. After further research, I have realized that this is often the pattern of modern anti-Mormon arguments, especially against Joseph Smith. They manipulate the story by only sharing certain portions, or their sources come from those who are trying to destroy the Church or those who even helped kill Joseph Smith.

I genuinely believe that any decent person who seriously studies the Prophet's life through credible primary sources—including the writings of Joseph himself—cannot honestly say that Joseph Smith was anything but a truthful, virtuous, and incredible man, even if that person does not believe he was truly a prophet of God. One of the main goals of this book is to tell the real story, while making it simple to read and understand. *1,001 Facts about the Prophet Joseph Smith* is a history book for this generation. The entire book can be read in one sitting, or readers can jump around to different moments in the Prophet's life and learn about their favorite and the most fascinating events. I wrote it using only primary accounts to make it as accurate as possible. This book is not meant to portray Joseph Smith as a perfect man; then *I* would be a liar. This book is meant to show Joseph Smith as the man he really was—as accurately as possible—based on primary sources. This book contains the *real* story.

ANCESTORS AND FAMILY OF THE PROPHET

1. One of Joseph Smith's ancestors was named John Howland. John Howland was a Puritan who traveled to America in pursuit of religious freedom on the Mayflower. This is how Joseph's family came to the United States.

2. Joseph Smith Sr., the Prophet's father, was born on July 12, 1771, in Topsfield, Essex County, Massachusetts. He died at the age of sixty-nine on September 14, 1840. He passed away four years before his sons Joseph, Hyrum, and Samuel Harrison, and sixteen years before his wife, Lucy. She died on May 14, 1856.

3. Joseph Smith Sr. was the third child in a family of eleven children. His parents were Asael and Mary Duty Smith.

4. Both of the Prophet's grandfathers, Asael Smith and Solomon Mack, fought with the American colonists in the Revolutionary War. Solomon Mack, the Prophet's maternal grandfather, enlisted with his two sons, Jason and Stephen.

5. The Prophet's mother, Lucy Mack Smith, was born on July 8, 1777, one year and four days after the United States Declaration of Independence was signed. She was brought to this earth when the freedom of religion was possible for the first time ever. Just in time for the Restoration of the fulness of the gospel of Jesus Christ, which was brought forth by her son Joseph.

6. Lucy was born in Gilsum, Cheshire County, New Hampshire, to Solomon and Lydia Gates Mack.

7. After the Revolutionary War, Solomon Mack Sr. returned home and struggled for four years to obtain property. He was absent from his family during this time. When he finally came home, he was completely

broke. He vowed to instead dedicate his life to his family and the service of God.

8. Lydia Gates Mack was a school teacher. She had eight children with Solomon Mack. In one of the towns where the family resided, there were not any schools around for the children to attend. Instead, Lydia educated her children at home.

9. The Prophet's maternal uncle Daniel Mack was very courageous. He had three friends who went swimming in a river once. Daniel refused to swim with them because it would be too dangerous. His friends became overpowered by the river's current, and Daniel Mack jumped in and saved all three of them. They were so grateful that they all said they wanted to live their whole lives near him, and they did.

10. Lucy's oldest brother, Jason Mack, became a preacher at age twenty. He spent much of his life believing that by prayer and faith, God would one day manifest His power through revelations as He had anciently done. He was right; it was fulfilled in his nephew Joseph Smith Jr.!

11. Joseph's uncle Solomon Mack Jr. was the third son in the family and named after his father. Joseph Smith Jr. was also the third son in his family and named after his father.

12. Before she met and married Joseph Smith Sr., Lucy had a lot of anxiety about religion. She wanted to find the true church, but she was really confused about which to join. They all were so different from the original church of Christ and constantly criticizing each other. This is similar to how Joseph felt before he received his First Vision.

13. Lucy often went to pray in groves near her house even before she lived in Palmyra. It is likely that Joseph learned to pray seriously in the woods from his mother's example.

14. Many people do not know that Joseph Smith Sr. was actually a very talented music teacher. He had a beautiful singing voice. His musical talents were passed down to some of his children, including William and Don Carlos. They often sang together at conferences and other Church meetings later in life.

LUCY MACK SMITH OFTEN PRAYED IN GROVES NEAR HER HOUSE, EVEN BEFORE JOSEPH WAS EVER BORN.

15. Joseph Smith Sr. and Lucy Mack Smith were married on January 24, 1796.

16. Together Joseph Smith Sr. and Lucy Mack Smith had ten children: Alvin (February 11, 1798–November 19, 1824), Hyrum (February 9, 1800–June 27, 1844), Sophronia (May 16, 1803–July 22, 1876), Joseph Smith Jr. (December 23, 1805–June 27, 1844), Samuel Harrison (March 13, 1808–July 30, 1844), Ephraim (March 13, 1810–March 24, 1810), William (March 13, 1811–November 13, 1893), Katharine (July 28, 1812–February 1, 1900), Don Carlos (March 25, 1816–August 7, 1841), Lucy (July 18, 1821–December 9, 1882). Samuel Harrison, Ephraim, and William all share the same birthday.

17. Unfortunately, Joseph's little brother Ephraim only lived for twelve days.

18. All of Lucy and Joseph Smith Sr.'s children were tall, bulky, and strong, especially the boys.

19. Later in life, Joseph's younger sister Katharine could not financially care for one of her sons anymore. Joseph's older sister, Sophronia, raised Katharine's son as her own.

20. Katharine Smith (later Katharine Smith Salisbury Younger) lived longer than any of Lucy and Joseph Sr.'s other children. She died in the year 1900 at ninety-six years old.

21. While living in Randolf, Maine, after she had Alvin and Hyrum, Lucy became extremely ill. The doctors said she was going to die. She made a promise to God that she would serve Him the best she could if He would let her survive this illness. She heard a voice say to her that she would be healed because she faithfully asked God. She was healed in just a few moments. After this, she became consumed with the subject of religion and began her search for the truth. Eventually she realized that she felt there was not a true religion on earth at the time, so she relied on the teachings in the Holy Bible.

22. Before he joined The Church of Jesus Christ of Latter-day Saints, Joseph Smith Sr. was a universalist. Universalism is not an organized religion. The central belief, though, is that all people will go to heaven regardless of their beliefs or religion.

23. Both Lucy and Joseph Smith Sr. received several symbolic and religious visions through dreams, even before the Restoration of the gospel. None of their visions were as big and grand as Joseph's, though. Early in his

marriage to Lucy, Joseph Smith Sr. had a dream almost identical to the vision of the tree of life found in 1 Nephi 8 of the Book of Mormon. However, in Joseph Sr.'s dream, he was experiencing it with his own family members and children.

24. When the Smith family was living in Tunbridge, Vermont, Joseph Smith Sr. heard of a new way to earn a lot of money quickly. He heard that crystallized ginseng sold for a lot of money in China since it was a common remedy for the plague. He spent a lot of time crystallizing and exporting it. When he had enough, a merchant named Stevens offered him $3,000 for it, only two-thirds of the real value. Joseph Smith Sr. decided to ship it himself instead. Unfortunately, when Mr. Stevens found out where and how Joseph Smith Sr. was shipping his materials, he arranged for his son to ship his ginseng on the same ship.

25. The ginseng did sell for a lot of money in China, but Mr. Stevens said the Smiths only made a chest of tea, and that's what he gave them as payment. However, he drunkenly admitted to Lucy's brother Major Mack that Joseph Smith Sr. actually made a lot of money in China and it was in Mr. Stevens's possession. He even showed Major Mack the money. After sobering up, he fled to Canada with the money, never to be seen by the Smith family again.

26. This instance put the Smiths in a lot of debt. They sold their Tunbridge farm for $800 and added Lucy's dowry of $1,000 to cover the debt without any further issues.

27. Joseph Smith Jr.'s sister Sophronia almost died from typhus fever in New Hampshire. Distraught, Lucy paced back and forth, carrying her daughter in her arms and praying for her recovery. At one point, Sophronia even stopped breathing, but she recovered and eventually returned to full health from her mother's care and prayers.

28. When the Smith family lost their property in Tunbridge, they moved around for several years trying to obtain property and a permanent home. They lived in Pennsylvania, New Hampshire, and Vermont. Joseph Smith Sr. farmed in Norwich for a few years, but his crops continuously failed. Then they finally moved to Palmyra, New York, where the golden plates were deposited in the Hill Cumorah and Joseph received his First Vision.

29. Joseph Smith Sr. had to go to Palmyra first to clear up some financial misunderstandings. He sent a wagon team, which the Smiths owned, to help Lucy and the children move to New York.

30. One day, on their way to Palmyra, the leader of the wagon team, Mr. Howard, tried abandoning Lucy and the kids. In the morning, he threw their belongings off the wagons and was about to leave with the team. He asserted that he had spent all the Smiths' money and could not take them further. Lucy turned to the team and told them Mr. Howard's plans. She forbade them to go with Mr. Howard because the Smith family owned the wagons. Lucy fired Mr. Howard and led the team (and her eight children) to Palmyra by herself.

31. In order to obtain the farm in Palmyra, Lucy started her own business and actually did pretty well. She painted oil-cloth coverings for tables and stands. She completely furnished their new home using her business earnings alone.

LUCY MACK SMITH OWNED A BUSINESS SELLING PAINTED OIL-CLOTH COVERINGS.

32. Lucy and Joseph Smith Sr. prayed and sang hymns with their children every morning and night, even before Joseph Jr.'s First Vision. Because the family was very consistent and faithful in their religious practices, Joseph's younger brother William stated that he found the family's daily religious activities to be annoying.

33. In her autobiography, Lucy Mack Smith wrote that many people assume she has many phenomenal stories about Joseph's childhood before his First Vision. She claims that nothing out of the ordinary happened during Joseph's early life that was interesting enough to share—no crazy visions or miracles. Lucy and the rest of the Smith family were not trying to prove anything by exaggerating stories or making things up. If they were, there would be a lot more dramatic and fantasized stories from Joseph's early life that Lucy would want to share.

JOSEPH'S YOUTH

34.   Joseph Smith Jr. was born on December 23, 1805. For historical context, he was born only one month after Lewis and Clark reached the Pacific Ocean on their expedition.

35.   Joseph Smith Jr. was born on farm property owned by his maternal grandfather, Solomon Mack.

36.   Many believe the birth of the first latter-day prophet would be a day full of miracles, visions, heavenly signs, and the like, similar to the signs and miracles that occurred when Jesus Christ was born. This was not the case. Joseph Smith Jr.'s birth was nothing out of the ordinary. In fact, in Lucy's autobiography, she writes about Joseph's birth in only two sentences. He was an ordinary man who was later called by God to bring forth Christ's restored gospel.

37.   The doctor who delivered Joseph Smith Jr. was Dr. Joseph Adam Denison. Years later, he wrote that he wished he knew back then to kill the baby so he could never grow up to found the Church.

38.   When the Prophet was about seven years old, the Smith family was living in New Hampshire. Several members of the family became sick with typhus fever, caused by the typhoid epidemic in the area. After Joseph recovered from the illness, he had a very painful fever sore on his shoulder. The doctor cut a slit into it, which caused the pain to quickly travel down to Joseph's lower left leg.

39.   With modern medical knowledge and technology, doctors and scientists have concluded that the disease on Joseph's leg was osteomyelitis. Osteomyelitis still affects some people today.

40.   The severe pain in his leg produced extreme swelling over the next three weeks.

41. During the first two weeks, Joseph's mother carried him around so he did not have to walk and hurt himself. She worked so hard to take care of him that it made her sick from stress and overexertion. Hyrum took over, caring for Joseph and carrying him around.

JOSEPH SMITH JR. WAS BORN ON HIS GRANDFATHER'S FARM IN DECEMBER.

42. Hyrum would sit at Joseph's bedside and hold his leg in between his hands to help him bear the pain.

43. At first, the doctor made a small incision in the leg, which alleviated the pain until the wound started to heal. Then the pain came back, worse than before. The doctors tried this twice, with the same results.

44. After the second incision failed to correct the problem, Joseph's parents requested a council of surgeons, who decided the only way to fix Joseph's leg was to amputate it. At the time, it was the only proven cure to save his life. Back then, amputations were brutal. They were only performed as a last resort and required several men to hold down the completely conscious patient. Sometimes the operation was so severe that it killed the patient anyway.

45. Lucy begged the surgeons not to amputate her son's leg. She pleaded with them to just try cutting out the diseased part, as a last-ditch effort before removing the leg. She would not even let them into Joseph's room without first hearing them promise to try saving the leg. The doctors decided to try her suggestion.

46. At this time, eleven-year-old Hyrum Smith was attending Moor's Charity School, which was associated with Dartmouth College. He returned home sick. He knew of a doctor teaching at the Dartmouth medical school named Dr. Nathan Smith. Nathan Smith was the fifth graduate from Harvard Medical School with a bachelor's degree in medical science. He would eventually be the man in the council of surgeons to save Joseph Smith Jr.'s leg.

47. Many historians believe Dr. Nathan Smith to be the only man in the world who was capable of doing such a complicated, unproved surgery on the seven-year-old boy.

48. During this time, surgeries were generally done at the patient's home, on their own bed, without anesthesia. It resulted in agonizing pain for the patient.

49. The doctors said Joseph needed to be tied down during the procedure, and they offered him some liquor to take the edge off the pain. Seven-year-old Joseph refused to do either. He said that he would instead let his father hold him in his arms on the bed, completely conscious and sober, while the surgeons cut into his leg.

50. Joseph did not want his mom to have to watch him experience the excruciating pain. He asked her to leave the house so she would not have to witness or hear it. He also reassured her that God would help him.

51. The surgeons removed one large piece of bone from Joseph's small tibia, and then they removed fourteen additional pieces from the bone after removing the largest chunk.

52. Even though Lucy walked several hundred yards away from the house, she heard Joseph screaming loudly in pain when the first piece of bone was removed. She immediately ran back to the house and into Joseph's room. Joseph urged her to leave and promised to tough it out if she would go. She left but heard him cry in pain again. She ran inside to see Joseph's leg wound wide open and the bed covered in blood. Joseph was pale and sweating excessively. She had to be forced out of the room and detained until the operation was over.

53. In the months following the surgery, Lucy Mack Smith carried Joseph around the house so he would not put weight on his recovering leg. Eventually, he was able to start using crutches, and then he was able to walk without any assistance.

54. Joseph gradually made a full recovery, minus suffering from a slight limp for the rest of his life with one leg a little shorter than the other from the surgery.

55. Joseph Smith was never subject to military duties in any state. He was exempt due to his limp.

56. Amputation was still the main treatment for osteomyelitis until the First World War. Joseph's leg surgery was a miracle and unheard of at the time.

57. The leg operation performed on Joseph Smith would not be completed successfully on another patient until the early 1900s.

58. While living in Vermont, young Joseph would often gaze at the beauty of nature and wonder about the vastness of the sky and universe. He knew that God must have created it; this regularly strengthened his testimony of God's existence and power.

59. Joseph was still recovering from his leg surgery when he and his family moved to New York. On the way there, he was riding in the sleigh when the driver knocked him off. He was left behind, bloody and unable to stand up and walk the rest of the way himself. Luckily, a stranger was walking by and found Joseph. He carried Joseph to Palmyra to be reunited with his extremely worried family.

60. The Prophet was ten years old when the family moved to Palmyra, New York.

61. Wrestling was a popular activity in the Smith family during Joseph's youth. It was one of the favorite family games, especially among the boys.

62. The Smith family was not wealthy. Every member of the family had to work on the farm in Palmyra to help support their large family. They were not financially able to go to school. Joseph claimed he could read without much difficulty, write a little, and he understood the basics of mathematics. Many estimate that his education was equivalent to that of a child in third grade.

> MANY ESTIMATE THAT JOSEPH SMITH HAD THE EQUILAVENT OF A THIRD-GRADE EDUCATION.

63. Lucy Mack Smith once said that of all her children, Joseph was the least inclined to read books.

64. Joseph and his brothers' job on their father's New York farm was to plow and cultivate the soil for the crops. His sisters helped Lucy with indoor chores like cooking and cleaning. They all worked from day to night, six days a week.

65. Before Joseph was physically able to help his father and brothers in the fields, he helped his mother and sisters with their duties. Aside from helping cook and clean, whenever there was a big town gathering, Joseph took his family's pies and other goodies on a handmade cart and sold them to the other citizens. He helped support the family that way.

THE FIRST VISION

66. Beginning around the year 1818, several religious leaders in Palmyra began to rise in popularity. They contended against each other about which of their churches was correct. The members of these churches argued with members of other churches frequently as well. The conflict seemed never-ending.

67. During the religious excitement, Lucy Mack Smith and three of her children—Hyrum, Samuel Harrison, and Sophronia—joined the Presbyterian church.

68. It is believed that Joseph Smith Jr. had at least one family relative in every denomination in Palmyra.

69. Joseph did attend the different church meetings whenever he could, but he was never sure about joining any of them.

70. Joseph claimed that during this time, he felt he believed most of the doctrines taught in the Methodist sect, but he was still not completely convinced. The constant religious clash around the town led to a lot of confusion, especially in Joseph Smith Jr.'s mind. He really wanted to make sure he did what was right and joined the true church, but he did not know which was true. He did not know how he would ever find out the truth.

71. One day, while reading the Holy Bible, Joseph read James 1:5, which reads, "If any of you lack wisdom, let him ask of God, that giveth to all men liberally, and upbraideth not; and it shall be given him." He expressed that no passage of scripture had ever been so powerful to him. He decided that if he wanted answers, he needed to ask God which church to join.

72. In the spring of 1820, he went to a grove of trees (now referred to by Latter-day Saints as "the Sacred Grove") near his father's farm to pray

privately for an answer about which church to join. He had never before made an attempt to pray out loud.

73. Joseph decided on a specific location in the Sacred Grove to pray before he went there. He had been planning it for a while and took it very seriously. However, he likely never expected what happened next.

74. Almost immediately after Joseph kneeled to pray in the woods, he heard what sounded like footsteps coming toward him from behind. He looked to see if somebody was there but found nobody. He tried praying again. The footsteps grew louder and louder, as if getting closer to him. He sprung to his feet and looked around again, but found nothing that could have caused the sound of footsteps. He knelt once more.

JOSEPH HAD NEVER TRIED TO PRAY OUT LOUD BEFORE GOING TO THE SACRED GROVE.

75. Joseph was then seized upon and overcome by a strong force or being that he could not physically see. His tongue swelled and seemed stuck to the roof of his mouth. He could not speak.

76. He had to try hard to pray, using all of his strength. His mouth and tongue were finally freed so he could speak again.

77. Once he could speak, he began his prayer. Then, he saw a pillar of light. The light looked like fire. At first it seemed like the "fire" was going to destroy the trees around him. Joseph was afraid and almost ran away until he realized the light was not burning the grove at all. So he stayed.

78. The light descended gradually until it rested on him. According to Alexander Neibaur's journal entry regarding Joseph's account of the First Vision, Joseph saw one personage, with fair complexion and blue eyes, come down in the light. This personage was God the Father.

79. The next personage, Jesus Christ, came down next to the first. He resembled the other in both "features and likeness," like how a son would resemble the features and likeness of his father.

80. The two personages' brightness and glory are impossible to explain. Their countenances, as well as the light they stood in above Joseph in the air, were brighter than the sun at noon day.

81. When the light surrounded Joseph, he was filled with the Spirit of God; it was so strong that he said it sent a shock throughout his entire body.

82. The first personage spoke to the young prophet while pointing to the second, "Joseph, this is my beloved son. Hear Him!"

83. What was the first known word spoken by God to any of his earthly children in this dispensation? "Joseph."

84. Along with these two personages, Joseph also saw angels. Many Latter-day Saints have wondered who else would have been permitted to accompany the Father and Son as angels in this vision.

85. In the Sacred Grove, Jesus Christ told the young boy that all his sins were forgiven of him.

86. Joseph asked the two personages if he should join the Methodist church. They said no. He then asked which church was true, so that he could join it. The answer he received was that he should join none of the churches, because they were all corrupt. Jesus Christ told him that the fulness of His gospel was about to be restored. If Joseph would keep the commandments and prepare himself, then he would be an instrument in bringing forth the fulness of the gospel.

87. Before asking in prayer which church he should join, it never occurred to him that all the churches on the earth at the time were incorrect.

88. Joseph claims that the personages told him many other things that he could not reveal at the time of recording. It is generally believed that he never revealed these things during his life, or at least not in writing.

89. When the vision was over, Joseph found himself sprawled on his back. Joseph felt like he had no physical strength for a little while after his vision. This turned out to be very common with his visions later in life as well. For example, the morning after the angel Moroni first visited him, Joseph passed out while walking home from working in the fields due to extreme spiritual and mental exhaustion.

90. Just a few months before his visitation from Heavenly Father and Jesus Christ, Joseph was out on an errand for his parents. He was just about to reach the house on his way home when he heard a gun being fired in his direction two times. Somebody was trying to shoot him. He was frightened and quickly ran inside. The family went outside later to try finding the shooter, but they failed.

91. They did find the tracks in the snow where the shooter hid under a wagon. The next morning, they found two balls in the head and neck of a cow nearby, which the shooter hit instead of Joseph. They never found the shooter and never learned why someone tried to randomly kill the

fourteen-year-old farm boy. This was before Joseph received persecution for the First Vision. To the Smith family, the motive of the attempted murderer was a total mystery.

92. Joseph went home after his vision in the Sacred Grove. He stood near the fireplace, unusually quiet. When his mother asked him why he was so somber, he replied assuring her that he was fine but that he learned for himself that the Presbyterian church (the church she and three of her children had joined) was wrong. It was a very interesting thing to say to his mother after seeing Heavenly Father and Jesus Christ in practically his own backyard.

93. A few days after Joseph saw the Father and the Son in the Sacred Grove, he went to his Methodist preacher and told him about his visitation. The preacher responded that there were no visions or revelations anymore. He said that Joseph's vision was all from the devil because visions and revelations ceased with the deaths of the original Twelve Apostles. This was the beginning of Joseph's persecution in Palmyra.

MANY EARLY SAINTS NEVER KNEW ABOUT JOSEPH'S EXPERIENCE IN THE SACRED GROVE.

94. Joseph Smith did not speak about the First Vision very often. In fact, many of the early Saints never learned about Joseph's First Vision during his lifetime. Joseph knew how sacred his story was, and he took it very seriously. Another reason he kept the First Vision mostly private was that telling the story almost always led to persecution. He learned this lesson for the first time after telling his Methodist preacher only a few days after the visitation.

95. It is not clear when he told his family about his vision or which family member Joseph told first. His family likely knew soon after it occurred, but they did not speak of it frequently either. That is probably why there is no documentation of their initial reactions and feelings.

96. Many modern nonbelievers challenge Joseph Smith's First Vision account, claiming that there is evidence that the Smith family was not yet in Palmyra in 1820. However, in 1819, Joseph Smith Sr. and Alvin Smith sued a man in Palmyra for selling them horses that almost immediately died after the purchase. The horses were not healthy enough to be sold to a couple of farmers who needed them for farm work. Joseph and Hyrum had to testify in court for this case. The court

record was recently discovered by historians. It therefore disproves any theories that the Smith family did not live in Palmyra by 1820.

97. All of the religious sects in Palmyra only seemed united on one thing: persecuting Joseph Smith. As word spread around town of Joseph's vision, Joseph and the Smith family endured more and more opposition.

98. The constant persecution from religious leaders made him wonder why people of such education and power would think that an obscure fourteen-year-old boy would be important enough to persecute so heavily.

99. Through all this trial from persecution, Joseph Smith often took comfort in the story of Paul in the Bible. Like Joseph Smith, Paul had to defend his visions before powerful people (in Paul's case, it was King Agrippa) who called him a liar. Yet it did not change the fact that Paul, like Joseph, beheld a vision. Joseph knew that because both he and God knew of his vision, he could never deny it without upsetting God, and he never did.

100. There are nine known written accounts of the First Vision. There are four firsthand accounts of Joseph himself and there are five accounts recorded by those who heard the Prophet speaking about his experience.

101. The first of the four firsthand accounts was written in the summer of 1832. It is the most personal account and is the only one that features Joseph Smith's handwriting. The others were written completely by his scribes. The next account was written after Joseph told the story of the First Vision to a Jewish man who was visiting his Kirtland home in 1835. It was written down and later copied to Joseph's journal. The third account is the most well-known. It is found today in the Pearl of Great Price. The last firsthand account was prepared at the request of a Chicago newspaper editor. It was published with Joseph's signature. This account is also nicknamed "the Wentworth Letter."

> THERE ARE NINE KNOWN WRITTEN ACCOUNTS OF THE FIRST VISION.

102. The first of the five secondhand accounts was written by Orson Pratt in 1840. It was published as a pamphlet that circulated throughout Scotland.

103. The next account was written by Orson Hyde at first in English, and then he translated it into German so it could be published in Frankfurt in 1842.

104. The third of the secondhand accounts can be found in Levi Richards's journal in 1843, which he wrote after hearing the Prophet speak about it in church.

105. The fourth secondhand account was published in 1843 by David Nye White in the *Pittsburg Weekly Gazette* article titled, "The Prairies, Joe Smith, The Temple, The Mormons, &c." During his interview with Joseph Smith in Nauvoo, White recorded what Joseph said about his vision.

106. The final account is found in the journal of Alexander Neibaurn on May 24, 1844, about one month before the Prophet's death. Neibaurn visited Joseph's home and listened to his story seeing God the Father and Jesus Christ in the Sacred Grove, and he wrote about it in his journal.

107. Each account of the First Vision is told with slight differences. Joseph Smith's story never changed. However, he would focus on different elements of the story based on who was listening. For example, in 1835, a Jewish man visited the Prophet's home in Kirtland, Ohio. When Joseph told the First Vision story to this man, it seems that he did not mention seeing Jesus Christ; he only mentioned that he saw God. This is probably because the man did not believe that Jesus was the Messiah and therefore would not benefit from hearing the full story.

108. Besides his First Vision account, Joseph also included a list of Latter-day Saint beliefs to disprove any confusion or rumors circulating at the time about the Saints in the Wentworth Letter. Today, we call them the Articles of Faith.

ANGEL MORONI VISITATIONS

109. In the few years following Joseph Smith's First Vision, through all the persecution, he fell into temptations. He became guilty of things he felt were unacceptable for one who had been called of God. However, he stated that he never committed any "malignant sins" and that those types of sins were "never in [his] nature." He claimed that he was guilty of levity and engaging with "jovial company." It basically means that he tended to be lighthearted and silly, and he believed that a man called of God needed to be more sedated and serious (Joseph Smith, in *History of the Church*, 1:133).

110. Three years after Joseph Smith's First Vision, on the night of September 21, 1823, Joseph knelt to pray before going to bed. Joseph was praying for forgiveness for his sins. He was also asking to know where he stood with God at that time and to speak with a messenger who could answer his questions.

111. On this night, Joseph was seventeen years old. He was three months and two days away from turning eighteen years old.

112. While he was praying, a light appeared. At first, it seemed like the house would be consumed with fire, which produced a shock that affected his entire body. It is not clear from the record if this was because of fear, or from being filled with the Spirit of God in order to see such a heavenly vision.

113. A heavenly messenger appeared in this light in his bedroom. He said his name was Moroni.

114. The angel Moroni stood above Joseph in the air; his feet did not touch the ground. Joseph described his brightness and glory like that of lightning. He had on a loose white robe and wore nothing on his hands and feet. His robe had the appearance of having no seam.

115. Moroni's countenance and presence brought peace to Joseph. He had no fear at all when Moroni visited him.

116. The light surrounding Moroni was so radiant that it made the whole room brighter than at noon day.

117. Joseph shared a room with his siblings at the time. However, they all slept through this visitation.

118. The heavenly messenger informed Joseph that the Native Americans were literal descendants of Abraham. He gave Joseph a brief explanation of their history, origin, civilizations, governments, and their relationship with God.

119. The angel Moroni told Joseph of an ancient record kept by his Native American ancestors, which contained the fulness of the gospel. The gospel's fulness was delivered by Jesus Christ to the ancient American people.

JOSEPH'S SIBLINGS ALL SLEPT THROUGH THE ANGEL MORONI'S VISITATIONS.

120. The record was written on golden plates. They were buried by Moroni himself hundreds of years prior.

121. Each gold plate was about six inches wide and eight inches long. The entire volume of plates was about six inches thick.

122. Deposited with the plates were two stones with silver bows. There was also a breastplate.

123. The stones were called the Urim and Thummim. They were used as seers in ancient times. God prepared them for the translation of the gold plates in the latter days.

124. The Urim and Thummim were two transparent stones. They were each approximately forty millimeters (about an inch and a half) in diameter.

125. Joseph learned during this visitation that he was going to be God's instrument in translating the record if he would be faithful and keep the commandments.

126. The angel revealed that both good and evil would be spoken of Joseph Smith among all people around the world. This statement is still true today.

127. Moroni showed Joseph in a vision where the plates were deposited. The phenomenon was so vivid and distinct that Joseph knew the place again when he saw it in real life.

128. Moroni quoted several scriptures from the Old Testament. He recited part of Malachi 3 and Malachi 4, with a little variation from how it was written in the Bible at the time.

129. He quoted Isaiah 11, asserting that it was about to be fulfilled. Moroni also quoted Acts 3:22–23 exactly as they read in the Bible. The messenger stated that the prophet in this chapter was Christ, but the time had not yet come. He lastly quoted Joel 2:28 through the end of the chapter. Moroni said that the prophecy had not been fulfilled but was about to be. The fulness of the Gentiles was soon to come. The angel Moroni said many more things that Joseph could not reveal.

130. Moroni appeared to Joseph three times that night, repeating the exact same message. On the second visitation, Moroni added information about the great judgements coming to this generation on the earth. On the third visitation, Moroni cautioned Joseph to beware of covetousness when getting the plates. They were not to be used for financial gain. Joseph was only to translate them.

JOSEPH WAS COMMANDED TO TELL NO ONE ABOUT HIS VISION EXCEPT HIS FATHER, JOSEPH SMITH SR.

131. Moroni warned Joseph not to show anybody the plates, stones, or the breastplate unless Heavenly Father commanded him to do so.

132. Moroni then commanded him to tell his father about all that he saw and heard in this vision.

133. After the angel finished relaying his message, the light went out except just surrounding Moroni, and then a passage opened into heaven. Moroni ascended into it.

134. Joseph was not aware of anything else around him except the vision, which is why he did not realize it was morning when the vision was over. The conversation between Joseph and Moroni lasted all night.

135. The next morning, Joseph, his brother Alvin, and Joseph Smith Sr. were working in the field. Joseph seemed exhausted and kept losing focus. Joseph Sr. noticed this and thought his son looked pale and sick. He told him to go to home and rest.

136. On Joseph's way back to the house, he passed out from exhaustion. He was too weak to stand. The angel Moroni appeared to Joseph again and asked, "Why did you not tell your father that which I commanded you to tell him?" Joseph responded, "I was afraid my father would not believe me." Moroni comforted him, saying, "He will believe every word you say to him" (Lucy Mack Smith, *The History of Joseph Smith by His Mother*, 79).

137. Joseph went back to the field to find that his father had gone back to the house, feeling sick as well. He asked Alvin to go get him because Joseph had something very important to tell him.

138. When Joseph Sr. returned, the young prophet told him everything he saw and heard the night before. His father believed him, told him it was of God, and instructed him to go immediately to the spot where the plates were buried.

139. The plates were buried a short distance from the Smith family farm. They were found in a place now called Hill Cumorah, as it was referred to in ancient times by the Nephites and Lamanites.

140. The Hill Cumorah is a large hill in Manchester, New York. The plates were hidden close to the top of the hill inside a stone box in the ground. This kept moisture from getting to the plates, seer stones, and breastplate. The hole in the ground was covered by a large rock. The rock's edges were covered in dirt.

141. When Joseph went there, he found a stick which he used as a lever. He wedged it under the large rock and pushed the rock to the side. Just like the angel Moroni had said, there Joseph found the gold plates, the Urim and Thummim, and the breastplate.

142. Moroni appeared again to Joseph at the Hill Cumorah. The angel showed him through a vision both the heavens and the adversary, along with the adversary's followers. He explained to Joseph that he was shown good and evil so he would know both and not be influenced by wickedness.

143. Moroni presented to Joseph the consequences of obedience and disobedience at the Hill Cumorah so he could remember to keep the commandments of God.

144. The heavenly messenger told Joseph that he was not ready to take the plates yet. They needed to wait until Joseph was both willing and able to take them and translate them. He was instructed to prepare by keeping

the commandments and returning to that same spot to meet Moroni at the same time every year for further instructions.

145. Oliver Cowdery visited the burial place of the plates with the Prophet years later in 1830. Cowdery stated that because the plates were deposited in the earth over one thousand years before Joseph received them, they were several feet below ground. He was unable to give the exact distance, but said the plates were considerably deep due to the natural wearing of the ground over time. However, since the plates were placed near the top of the hill, where the earth would not wear as severely and where the trees grew to cover the surface of the hill, it was not too deep for Joseph to reach. Regardless, he did have to dig a fairly large hole in the ground to get to the plates.

146. Looking for the stone box where the plates were buried? Unfortunately, around 1910, the man who owned the Hill Cumorah land was tired of people coming on his property to find the stone box. He put up a "No Trespassing" sign, destroyed the stone box, and filled in the hole in the ground so it could no longer be found.

THE OWNER OF THE HILL CUMORAH DESTROYED THE STONE BOX THAT THE PLATES WERE FOUND IN TO KEEP TRESSPASSERS AWAY.

147. That night, Joseph returned home. He told the rest of his family about the visions and the plates. They were excited, and they wanted to know every detail. Alvin, Joseph's oldest brother, noticed that the young prophet was exhausted from these events. He suggested that the family instead go to bed and let Joseph rest. They planned to finish their work in the field early the next day. Lucy planned to make dinner early, so then they could spend the rest of the evening listening to Joseph's visions and learning about him finding the plates.

148. This was a frequent family activity; they listened to new visions and revelations from Joseph as they came. As Joseph continued to receive further instructions from God, the family would gather every evening to listen to what Joseph had learned. Lucy once said, "I presume our family presented an aspect as singular as any that ever lived . . . all seated in a circle, father, mother, sons, and daughters, and giving the most profound attention to a boy, 18 years of age, who had never read the Bible through in his life" (Lucy Mack Smith, *The History of Joseph*

Smith by His Mother, 82). As the family learned more from Joseph, they became happier, more peaceful, and hopeful.

149. Every single member of the family believed in what Joseph had experienced because he was an honest person. The fact that the Smith family never once thought Joseph was lying says a lot about both the Smith family and the character of Joseph Smith himself.

150. Joseph warned his family members not to speak to others about what was revealed to him and about the plates. He said that if word got out about it, others would try to kill the Smith family.

151. In the evenings, when the family would gather to listen to Joseph, he would sometimes tell them about the ancient inhabitants of the Americas. He would explain their clothes, animals, buildings, cities, warfare, religious practices, etc. It seemed like he knew them as familiarly as he would know his lifelong friends.

PREPARING TO GET THE PLATES

152. On September 22, 1824, Joseph returned to the Hill Cumorah to see the plates and receive further instruction from the angel Moroni.

153. Since Joseph had been working hard to keep the commandments of God, he fully expected to take the plates home the first year he returned to the Hill Cumorah. That was not the case.

154. Joseph went to where they were buried and took the plates out. Then he thought about the possibility that something else could be in the stone box that he could use to become wealthy. He put the plates on the ground and paid no attention to them while he covered the box with dirt so nobody else would find it. Once he finished, he turned around to grab the plates—but they were gone.

155. He panicked and searched frantically for them. He immediately prayed to Heavenly Father, asking where the plates were and why they were gone. The angel Moroni appeared and told Joseph that he disobeyed the commandment to never put the plates down until he could place them in a chest with a good lock and key.

156. After this chastisement, Moroni allowed Joseph to lift the stone again to find the plates safely inside. Joseph tried to grab the plates, but he was violently thrown to the ground. He looked up to discover that the angel was gone. Joseph walked home in tears.

157. Once Joseph got home, his father asked if he had gotten the plates. Joseph said he had not. Joseph Sr. replied that if he were in his son's position, he would have taken the plates. Joseph had to explain to his father that the angel would not let him because he disobeyed God's commandment.

158. After the Smith family learned about what happened with Joseph and the plates, they worried that Joseph had ruined his chances of ever getting them. The entire family doubled their efforts in keeping the commandments in hopes that Joseph could still get the plates.

159. About three years before Joseph Smith Jr. could take the plates, Joseph Smith Sr. told a friend in confidence about Joseph's visions and about the golden plates. Eventually this friend accidentally let the word spread, which of course led to intense persecution on the Smith Family. This family friend's name was Martin Harris.

ALVIN'S DEATH

160. Alvin and Hyrum were Joseph's older brothers. They were Joseph's role models; he deeply admired both of them.

161. In November 1824, Joseph's oldest brother, Alvin, decided to build a bigger house for his parents. He wanted them to live a leisurely life in their old age. The house was only a few yards away from their current house. Alvin was not able to finish it before he died.

162. On November 15, 1824, Alvin became sick with a bilious colic, which is what we would refer to today as a gallbladder attack or gallstone attack.

163. At first, Alvin had to be treated by a physician other than the usual family doctor. The physician gave Alvin calomel to treat his symptoms. The calomel got lodged in his stomach, which caused even more pain.

ALVIN SMITH, JOSEPH'S OLDER BROTHER, DIED FROM A GALLBLADDER ATTACK.

164. Because of Alvin's worsening condition, he knew he was going to die. He requested to speak to each member of his family while he lay in bed close to death.

165. To Joseph, Alvin said, "I am now going to die, the distress which I suffer, and the feelings that I have, tell me my time is very short. I want you to be a good boy, and do everything that lies in your power to obtain the record. Be faithful in receiving instruction and in keeping every commandment that is given you. . . . Set an example for the children that are younger than yourself, and always be kind to father and mother" (Lucy Mack Smith, *The History of Joseph Smith by His Mother*, 86).

166. Alvin asked Hyrum to take care of the family as the new eldest. He told him to take over the responsibility of finishing the house for their parents so they would not have to work in their old age. Hyrum did finish the house in the years following.

167. The new Smith home that Alvin started and Hyrum finished was one of the first frame homes to be built in the neighborhood.

168. Alvin Smith died on November 19, 1824.

169. The clergyman performing the ceremony of Alvin's funeral announced that Alvin was going to hell because he was never baptized. It shocked the Smith family because they all believed Alvin to be the most noble and faithful of them all. This statement angered Joseph Smith Sr. and solidified his belief that there was no true church on the earth at the time. He believed that God would not force his sweet, innocent, honest son to hell for not being baptized.

170. Alvin was one of the most interested of the family members in what Joseph had to say about the record and ancient American inhabitants. At first after his death, talking about the work that Joseph was called to do made the family depressed, and they would cry. Eventually, though, they desired to listen to Joseph's revelations again.

171. In the months following Alvin's death, one of the religious leaders in the community tried uniting the differing sects in Palmyra, and some of Joseph's family members desired to go to church with him. Lucy asked Joseph if he wanted to go with them to the church meetings. Joseph responded that he would not stop them from going to any church they desired, but he would not join any of them. He also said that he could

take a Bible into the grove and learn more in two hours than they could by attending church meetings for two years.

172. Joseph then prophesied that a religious leader in the community of Palmyra, Deacon Jessup, would confiscate the one cow from a widow and her children just to secure a debt. The Smiths thought very highly of Deacon Jessup and did not want to believe Joseph. Joseph's prophecy was fulfilled one year later.

JOSIAH STOWELL

173. A man named Josiah Stowell wanted to hire Joseph to help work in his silver mine in Pennsylvania. He heard that Joseph was a hard worker who had the ability to discern objects normally invisible to the human eye.

174. At first, Joseph tried to refuse Stowell's offer because he did not believe it was a smart investment for Stowell. However, after Stowell begged Joseph for a while, Joseph agreed to come work for him.

175. Josiah Stowell really enjoyed having Joseph work in his silver mine. At one point, a minister came to Mr. Stowell's home, demanding that he fire Joseph because he was claiming visions and causing confusion in the neighborhood. Stowell refused, saying that Joseph was a good worker and that he did not care about what Joseph claimed he saw. Joseph kept working for Josiah Stowell for a while.

176. Joseph Smith's employment under Josiah Stowell is where the exaggerated stories and fallacies about Joseph being a "money digger" come from.

177. For a short time while Joseph was employed by Mr. Stowell, he lived with a man named Isaac Hale. This is where he met his future wife, Emma Hale.

EMMA HALE SMITH

178. Isaac Hale was married to Elizabeth L. Hale. Together they had nine children, Jesse, David, Alva, Isaac Ward, Rueben, Phebe, Tryal Morse, Elizabeth, and Emma.

179. Emma Hale was the seventh of their nine children.

180. Emma Hale was born on July 10, 1804. She was about a year and a half older than Joseph Smith.

181. The Hale family was very intelligent and respectable. They lived in Harmony, Pennsylvania, on the Susquehanna River.

182. Each of Emma's siblings attended traditional school. Emma was the only one of her siblings to do an extra year of schooling beyond that.

183. At one point, work at Josiah Stowell's slowed down a bit. Joseph lived with a man named Joseph Knight. Knight would let Joseph borrow his sleigh to go riding with Emma while they were courting.

184. Joseph was home in Palmyra one day when he pulled his parents aside to tell them that he had been very lonely since Alvin's death. He decided it was time for him to get married. He asked if his parents would have any objections to him marrying Emma Hale.

185. Lucy and Joseph Sr. were thrilled to hear this. In fact, they were so happy that they requested that he and Emma come live with them in New York.

186. Joseph Smith Sr. accompanied his son back to Harmony, Pennsylvania, so Joseph Jr. could get permission from Emma's father and ask her to marry him.

187. Since rumors and persecution always haunted Joseph, Emma's family was opposed to their marriage. Isaac Hale would not allow them to be married at his house. Instead, Joseph and Emma got married at Justice Zechariah Tarble's home in New York. Justice Zechariah Tarble officiated the wedding ceremony as well.

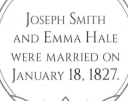

JOSEPH SMITH AND EMMA HALE WERE MARRIED ON JANUARY 18, 1827.

188. Joseph Smith Jr. and Emma Hale were married on January 18, 1827.

189. Lucy was excited to have Joseph and Emma come live with them. She spent the entire time that her husband and son were in Pennsylvania

working on the house to get it ready for Emma and Joseph's arrival. She had such a positive experience with Hyrum's first wife, Jerusha, that she was eager to have another daughter-in-law.

190. MYTH: Because Emma experienced so much trial in her lifetime, she was very pessimistic and complained often. FACT: The truth is the exact opposite. Emma was generally very cheerful and happy. Lucy Mack Smith once stated that Emma got extremely sick for four weeks. She said it was hard on Emma, but her spirits stayed the same. She said this was always how Emma's attitude was, even in the most trying circumstances throughout her life.

191. While Joseph and Joseph Smith Sr. were away in Pennsylvania, the carpenter who built the Smith family farm lied to the agent in charge of the home. He claimed the Smith family was not making payments to him for his work, even though they were paying him and had mutually agreed on a plan with the carpenter for the final payment. The agent believed the carpenter and bought the Smith family farm out from underneath them, basically evicting the Smith family. The Smiths had to move to the unfinished house that Hyrum was building for them.

192. One night while Joseph and Emma lived with the Smith family in Palmyra, Joseph was supposed to be home by six o'clock that night, but he did not return until hours later. Emma and the Smith family were extremely worried. Joseph came in and sat down. They asked him where he had been. He said that because he was not engaged enough in the Lord's work, he had just received the most severe chastisement yet from the angel Moroni. The angel told him to repent and keep the commandments so he could get the plates in September later that year.

193. Moroni told Joseph that if he did not strictly obey the commandments to prepare to receive the plates that September, he would lose his chance and never get them.

194. Joseph got the Urim and Thummim (the seer stones) first. Joseph's family, especially his wife and parents, knew he was going to try getting the stones one day. On that day, he decided to play a little joke on his family and Joseph Knight, who was staying at the Smith house. Joseph came inside the house, sat down, and put his head in his hands, suggesting that he was deeply saddened. The whole family seemed to feel bad for Joseph, fearing the angel did not let him get the seer stones yet. Joseph Knight tried comforting him, but then Joseph Smith cracked a smile, laughed, and told them that he actually succeeded in

getting the stones and that they were so much more amazing than he had imagined. Joseph Knight and the Smith family rejoiced.

195. In the few months before he got the plates, Joseph always carried the Urim and Thummim on his person. He could look at them anytime to see whether the plates were in danger or not.

196. To prevent other people from finding the plates—especially after rumors of "Joe Smith's gold Bible" began to circulate—Joseph had to remove them and hide them in another place on the Hill Cumorah before he was ready to take them home and translate them. He found a large decayed log. He cut a flat piece of the bark, big enough for the plates to fit through like a door. Then he cut a hole in the middle of the log that could fit the golden plates. He put the plates inside and replaced the bark door on top. To hide this area of the log as much as possible, he covered it with leaves, rocks, dirt, and anything else he could find nearby.

JOSEPH HID THE GOLD PLATES IN A LOG TO PROTECT THEM UNTIL HE WAS READY TO TRANSLATE THEM.

197. One day, Joseph Smith Sr. came home after speaking with a group of people who threatened to find and steal the plates from their hiding place, despite not knowing exactly where they were located. He spoke with Emma about his concerns. Emma replied that if Joseph was called of God to receive the plates, then he would succeed in getting them and no person or thing could stop it. Emma already had a strong testimony of the Lord's eternal plan and in Joseph as a prophet of God before he had even acquired the plates for translation.

198. Joseph Smith Sr. still shared his concern that Joseph might become like Esau in the Bible, who lost his birthright very easily. He desired to prevent that from happening at all costs. Emma rode one of the Smith family's horses to Joseph's workplace. She told Joseph all that had happened and of his family's worries. He checked the Urim and Thummim in his pocket and saw that the plates were safe. However, he went to get the plates that night to ensure they would remain protected.

GETTING THE PLATES

199. Before he took the plates, neither Joseph nor his parents had a chest with a good lock and key to put the plates in safely. They decided to have one made by a cabinetmaker who built some of their furniture, but Joseph did not have money to pay her. Emma, Joseph, and the family prayed about it. The following day, a local widow asked Joseph to work on a project in her well. This would provide the money they needed to pay the cabinetmaker for the chest.

200. Due to the dangerous threats from those who desired to take the plates, however, Joseph had to save the record before the chest was finished. Hyrum lent him a chest with a good lock and key.

201. When Joseph was getting the plates from the Hill Cumorah, Moroni appeared and warned him that wicked men would try every strategy possible to steal the plates from the Prophet. He cautioned Joseph that if he did not take heed continually, the wicked would succeed in taking them.

202. Before Joseph received the plates, the plates were protected in the Hill Cumorah by the angel Moroni. No man had power to take them away. Once Joseph took them, though, it was possible for wicked men to get ahold of them. Joseph listened to Moroni's warning and kept the plates safe so that wicked men never got the plates.

203. When Joseph got the plates, he had the impression that it would be safer to walk through the woods back to his house rather than taking the main road. He walked through the forest and was attacked three different times by three different men. Two of the men had guns. They did not try to shoot

> JOSEPH WAS ATTACKED IN THE WOODS THREE TIMES ON HIS WAY HOME AFTER RETRIEVING THE GOLD PLATES.

the Prophet, but they did strike him with the guns. Joseph was a large, muscular man. Each time he was attacked by these men in the woods, he pushed them off his body and onto the ground without losing any speed.

204. When he defended himself against the third attacker, he dislocated his thumb, but he did not even realize he was injured until he got home. Once the plates were safe, Joseph Smith Sr. put his son's thumb back in place.

205. Once Joseph got home with the plates, Joseph Smith Sr. and two other men (Mr. Knight and Mr. Stowell) went out to try finding the men who attacked the Prophet. The assaulters were never found.

206. In Orson Hyde's account of the First Vision, Hyde stated that Joseph Smith Jr. was once beaten so violently in Palmyra by two men with clubs that he bore the scars on his body for the rest of his life. The instance that Orson Hyde is speaking of is likely when Joseph was attacked multiple times on his way home from getting the plates on the Hill Cumorah. He was attacked so forcefully, yet he defended himself without dropping or losing the plates.

207. When Joseph came home from the Hill Cumorah with the plates, his twelve-year-old brother, Don Carlos, went to Hyrum's house next door to request the chest with a good lock and key. Hyrum was sitting at his table with his wife's two sisters, about to have tea. Just as Hyrum was putting his teacup to his mouth, Don Carlos put his hand on Hyrum's shoulder. Without Don Carlos saying a word, Hyrum knew immediately what was going on. He jumped up from the table, ran to grab his chest to lend to Joseph, emptied all its contents, and immediately left the house with the chest and the lock and key without saying one word. Hyrum's wife's sisters were extremely confused. They went to Hyrum's wife, Jerusha, and told her that Hyrum must be crazy. Jerusha explained that Hyrum must have instead just realized that he had forgotten something.

208. After bringing home the plates, Joseph moved back home to work on his father's farm and to be close to the plates and protect them.

209. On the day that Joseph brought home the breastplate, he had his mother hold it while he got the chest ready to put the breastplate in. It was wrapped in a cloth that was thin enough for her to easily feel its proportions. Lucy described it as "concave on one side, and convex on

the other, and extended from the neck downwards, as far as the center of the stomach of a man of extraordinary size. It had four straps of the same material, for the purpose of fastening it to the breast, two of which ran back to go over the shoulders, and the other two were designed to fasten to the hips . . . just the width of my two fingers (for I measured them), and they had holes in the end of them, to be convenient in fastening" (Lucy Mack Smith, *The History of Joseph Smith by His Mother*, 107).

210. After Joseph put the breastplate away safely, he asked Lucy if there were men walking around the house that day. Lucy said there were not any. He then prophesied that a mob was going to come by the house that night and try taking the plates. They needed to hide the plates quickly.

211. The Smith family dug up a portion of the brick floor of the fireplace, put the plates and the breastplate inside the ground, and replaced the bricks to hide them from the mob. As soon as they finished doing so, they looked outside to see a mob approaching the house.

212. Before the mob reached the Smith home, Joseph threw open the front door and yelled to get the attention of his family inside the house. Every male member of the Smith family, from Joseph Smith Sr. to the youngest brother Don Carlos, ran out toward the mob. This frightened the mob, even though they were not outnumbered. They retreated and returned to their homes.

213. On another occasion when Joseph received revelation of a mob coming to steal the plates, he ran across the farm to hide the plates in the floor of the cooper's shop. A cooper was somebody who built things such as barrels and utensils, usually made of wood.

TRANSLATING THE BOOK OF MORMON

214. Martin Harris was Joseph Smith's first scribe in translating the Book of Mormon. Joseph's scribes never saw the plates during translation. Joseph would sit with the plates behind a makeshift curtain and dictate to his scribes what the stones read from the plates. Both Oliver Cowdery and Martin Harris did see the plates later, though, as two of the three witnesses of the Book of Mormon.

215. Both Martin Harris and his wife repeatedly offered Joseph Smith money to help translate and publish the Book of Mormon. He always refused until finally he consented to accept $28 from Mrs. Harris to get her to stop insisting.

216. The persecution in Palmyra was getting so horrible that Joseph and Emma had to move to Pennsylvania to live with Emma's father, Isaac Hale, while Joseph translated.

217. While traveling to Pennsylvania to move in with his father-in-law, Joseph put the plates in a barrel of beans. He was stopped two different times by two different officers who ransacked his wagon, looking for the plates. They never found them.

218. The persecutors in Palmyra found out about Joseph's plans to move to Pennsylvania to safely translate the record. A mob of fifty men gathered to try to follow him and steal the plates. However, the mob argued so much about who would be their captain that they eventually broke up and went home.

219. The Urim and Thummim that Joseph used to translate the Book of Mormon were the same seer stones given to the brother of Jared in Ether 3 of the Book of Mormon.

> THE URIM AND THUMMIM ARE THE SAME SEER STONES THAT WERE GIVEN TO THE BROTHER OF JARED IN ETHER 3.

220. When Joseph used the seer stones to translate the record, he placed the stones in a spot where there was no light. Then, Joseph and his scribe would pray. The answer would appear in letters of light on the stones before disappearing again.

221. Sometimes after a long session of translating the plates, Joseph Smith and Martin Harris would go swim in the Susquehanna River for a little while to rest and rejuvenate. One time, Martin found a rock in the river basically identical to the Urim and Thummim. He put the rock in his pocket and later secretly switched it with one of the real seer stones. Joseph stared at the stones for over a minute in silence and then asked Martin what was wrong, why the stones were dark. Martin Harris confessed and switched the stones back. This instance really solidified Martin Harris's testimony that Joseph Smith was a prophet of God. If Joseph had been fabricating the Book of Mormon instead of translating it, he would have kept speaking. However, because Joseph really was translating the Book of Mormon and the seer stones really were from God and necessary for the translation, Joseph could not see God's translation through the random rock.

222. Once, Joseph copied the symbols over from the plates onto a separate piece of paper, along with their translation. In February 1828, Martin Harris brought those characters to a professor in New York named Charles Anthon. Charles Anthon was a highly educated man who was celebrated for his literary achievements and intelligence.

223. Professor Anthon examined the symbols with their translation. He stated that the translation was correct. In fact, he said it was more correct than any other Egyptian translations he had ever seen. Martin Harris also showed Professor Anthon some of the symbols that had not been translated yet. Anthon stated that they were true characters, written in Egyptian, Chaldeak, Assyriak, and Arabic.

> PROFESSOR CHARLES ANTHON CONFIRMED THAT A SAMPLE OF JOSEPH'S TRANSLATION OF THE SYMBOLS ON THE PLATES WAS CORRECT.

224. Professor Charles Anthon gave Martin Harris a certificate declaring that those symbols were in fact true characters and the translation of them was correct. Martin Harris put the certificate in his pocket and was about to leave the house when Anthon began to ask questions about the gold plates. Martin informed him that an angel of God revealed them to Joseph. The professor

immediately demanded to get the certificate back, and he ripped it to shreds.

225. Professor Anthon claimed that the ministering of angels did not exist and that Martin should bring the plates for Anthon to translate himself. Martin replied that some of the plates were sealed and he was forbidden to bring them. The professor replied, "I cannot read a sealed book." Both Isaiah and John prophesy in the Bible of an educated man asking to receive a book and, when denied, the man would say the words, "I cannot read a sealed book." The "sealed book" these prophets in the Holy Bible spoke about was the Book of Mormon (Joseph Smith, in *History of the Church*, 1:13).

226. After this, Martin Harris took the same characters to another highly educated and celebrated literary man named Dr. Samuel L. Mitchell. He also stated that the symbols were true characters and that Joseph's translation was correct.

LOST 116 PAGES

227. Martin Harris's wife, Lucy Harris, frequently tried sneaking a peek at the golden plates. Once, she came with her husband to where Joseph was living in Pennsylvania. She searched the entire house and could not find them. Instead, she investigated outside the house. She found an area where she was sure the plates had to be buried. She was about to start digging for them, when a big black snake slithered up to her and hissed. She ran away screaming, forcing her to give up her search. It was winter, and Emma later stated that there were normally no snakes in the area.

228. After this, Lucy Harris became bitter about the translation of the record and forbade Martin Harris from assisting from then on. He ignored her and helped Joseph translate anyway.

229. Martin Harris was Joseph Smith's first scribe in translating the Book of Mormon until the first 116 pages of the manuscript were lost.

230. After Martin Harris scribed the first 116 pages of the record, he asked Joseph if he could take the manuscript home to calm his skeptical wife's emotions about the situation.

231. Joseph asked the Lord regarding Martin's question three times. The first time, God said Joseph should not let Martin Harris take the manuscript home to his wife. When Martin Harris heard this, he asked Joseph to inquire again. Joseph did so and received the same answer from God. Martin begged Joseph to ask God one last time.

232. When Joseph prayed about it this time, he received the revelation that Martin could take the manuscript home only if he showed it to his wife and four other family members whom the Lord instructed Harris to show it to. Martin Harris promised to do as God asked.

233. Martin Harris was only supposed to show the manuscript to his wife, Lucy; his brother, Preserved; his father, Nathan; his mother, Rhoda; and his sister-in-law, Polly. He did so. However, when a close family friend visited Martin's home, Martin told him about the manuscript. This family friend was excited about it, and Martin Harris decided to show him the manuscript too.

234. Martin went to get the key to the chest holding the manuscript, but he could not find it. Instead, Martin picked the lock, grabbed the manuscript, and showed it to his friend. Eventually, both he and his wife showed the manuscript to several different people. One day when he checked for the manuscript in the chest, it was gone.

235. The same day that Martin Harris realized the manuscript had been stolen, a dense fog covered his fields and ruined two-thirds of his crops. However, the neighboring farms' crops had not suffered at all.

> WHEN MARTIN HARRIS LOST THE 116 PAGES, A DENSE FOG RUINED TWO-THIRDS OF HIS CROPS, BUT LEFT HIS NEIGHBORS' FARMS UNTOUCHED.

236. While Martin Harris had the manuscript at his house, Joseph and Emma's first child was born. They named him Alvin, after Joseph's late older brother. He died after a few hours. This sent Emma into a very depressive state. Joseph was worried after not hearing from Martin Harris in three weeks. However, he was too busy taking care of Emma to focus on it.

237. Eventually, Emma suggested that Joseph go to Martin Harris about the record and that he also send for her mother to come take care of her while she was in this depressive state.

238.	On his way to see Martin Harris, Joseph did not have the desire to eat or sleep because he was so afraid of what might have happened—and the consequences he would have to face because of it. There was one other man riding in the stagecoach with Joseph on the way to Martin Harris's home in Palmyra. When Joseph was leaving the stagecoach to walk the rest of the journey on foot, the man noticed that Joseph looked gloomy. He demanded to walk with the Prophet to his destination to make sure he was okay. The man walked Joseph the rest of the journey to the Harris home.

239.	Joseph panicked when he found out that the 116-page manuscript was lost. He feared that the Lord would never forgive him. He thought he ruined his chance to translate the rest of the record. The entire next day, Joseph did not eat. He cried and paced back and forth all day.

240.	The angel Moroni revealed to Joseph that the people who now had the manuscript intended to change the original so that it would not match the new, re-translated version. If Joseph were really translating the manuscript correctly, he would publish the same words again. But if the two versions were different, they could fool people into believing that Joseph Smith was fabricating the translation of the Book of Mormon. Joseph would not be able to re-translate the 116 pages.

241.	Instead, once he could translate again, he picked up where he left off. God knows all, though. Thousands of years previous, He commanded Nephi to record things that were already written in the record of his father, Lehi (translated on the first 116 pages). Nephi did not understand why the Lord commanded him to repeat information already written, but he obeyed. Because of this, the Book of Mormon is not missing any of the essential doctrine needed in these latter days.

242.	Moroni commanded Joseph to return the seer stones to him. Joseph would receive them again if he were to humble himself and repent.

243.	If Joseph were to re-translate the lost 116 pages the same as they were before written, wouldn't that prove to those who stole the manuscript that Joseph was honest and truly translating the record through the power of God? Why, then, did God still insist that Joseph not re-translate the lost 116 pages? The answer can be found in Doctrine and Covenants 10. The Lord reveals that the people who stole the manuscript were full of wickedness, corruption, and darkness. The adversary had so much influence over them, that they would have still tried to discredit Joseph as a prophet by changing the original manuscript so it would not match the re-translated version. It would not have mattered whether Joseph translated the same things as before or not, they still would not believe that he was a prophet of God.

244. Joseph and Martin were not the only ones who suffered from the loss of the 116 pages. Lucy Mack Smith said it affected the entire Smith family, that "the heavens seemed clothed with blackness, and the earth shrouded with gloom. I have often said within myself that if a continual punishment, as severe as that which we experienced on that occasion, were to be inflicted upon most wicked characters . . . if even their punishment were no greater than that, I should feel to pity their condition" (Lucy Mack Smith, *The History of Joseph Smith by His Mother*, 124).

RETURNING TO TRANSLATION

245. Joseph received the Urim and Thummim again from the angel Moroni after a period of serious repentance in the summer of 1828.

246. When Joseph received the gift to translate the record again, he did not immediately begin translating. He labored on a farm that he purchased from Emma's father. He needed to provide for his family first.

247. After losing the 116 pages, evidence from the original Book of Mormon manuscript suggests that Joseph translated the second half of the Book of Mormon first, and the first half after. He likely translated from Mosiah to the end of the book first (the larger plates), and then he translated 1 Nephi to Mosiah (the smaller plates).

248. The words in the original manuscript of the Book of Mormon are sort of crowded together in groups of about twenty-eight to thirty words. This suggests that Joseph could see twenty-eight to thirty words at a time while translating. He would dictate them to his scribe, and then they would move on to the next twenty-eight to thirty words.

JOSEPH COULD PROBABLY SEE ONLY TWENTY-EIGHT TO THIRTY WORDS AT A TIME WHILE TRANSLATING.

249. On average, they translated about twelve pages a day.

250. In March 1829, the Lord revealed to Joseph that there would be eleven more witnesses—the three witnesses and the eight witnesses—to the Book of Mormon once he finished the translation.

251. Emma was Joseph's scribe for a while. She could only write for him for short portions of the day, though.

252. Years after the Prophet's death, Emma told her son that while she was a scribe for Joseph Smith, he had no manuscripts, books, or notes as references during his dictations, or even around the house at all. She claims that if he did have anything like that, he could not have hidden them from her. Emma was an intelligent, educated woman and would not be easily fooled. She knew Joseph Smith better than most people ever will, and she knew he really translated the Book of Mormon.

253. Joseph prayed about needing another scribe so Emma could focus on her other responsibilities. The Lord promised Joseph that He would send another scribe to aid in the translation. Three days later, Oliver Cowdery, who had never met the Prophet before, arrived with Joseph's parents. Cowdery declared that the Lord had revealed to him that he should go to Joseph and be his new scribe.

254. Oliver Cowdery taught school in Palmyra and lived with Lucy and Joseph Smith Sr. while he was teaching. Cowdery heard rumors around town about the plates. Curious, he asked Joseph Sr. about them. Joseph Smith Sr. waited until he knew Oliver could be trusted to give him all the details regarding the plates and Joseph's role in translating them. After learning about the plates, Oliver thought about them all day and could not get them out of his mind. He had the impression that he should write for Joseph when school ended.

255. One night after Oliver Cowdery learned about the golden plates from Joseph Smith Sr., he prayed to know if what he was told was true. The Spirit told him that it was true. Oliver decided to keep this a secret, though. He told nobody about it. When the revelation in Doctrine and Covenants 6 was given to Joseph and Oliver, God mentioned to Oliver through the Prophet that Oliver was blessed for enquiring of the Lord and learning the truth (verses 14–17). He also gave Oliver further instructions regarding his mission as a scribe for Joseph. Since he had not spoken about his spiritual experience with any living person until then, Oliver Cowdery now knew that Joseph really was a prophet of God.

256. Oliver Cowdery loved the Smith family. When the Smiths moved from Palmyra to Manchester, Lucy told him they did not have room to house him anymore. He responded saying that he would live anywhere with them and never wanted to leave. He also called her "mother."

257. Oliver Cowdery arrived in Pennsylvania to translate for Joseph on April 5, 1829. They began translating the Book of Mormon two days after.

258. In the original manuscript of the Book of Mormon, there is a sequence of twenty-eight words written in Joseph Smith's handwriting. It is the earliest known record of the Prophet's handwriting. Some speculate that this was from when Oliver was once granted the opportunity to translate. Others believe that maybe Oliver was too tired late one night, so Joseph scribed the last twenty-eight words of the day himself.

259. The first time the name "Coriantumr" appears in the original Book of Mormon manuscript, it is misspelled as "Coriantumer." It is crossed out, with the correct spelling placed next to it. Since the correction was put immediately next to the original word, instead of above it, it means the correction was made immediately. Oliver Cowdery misspelled the name at first and then likely asked Joseph how to spell it. Joseph gave him a very unusual spelling. Oliver's spelling seems to make more sense to those who speak modern English. However, vowels were not used in some ancient languages, like Hebrew. The spelling of the name in Book of Mormon times makes perfect sense.

260. Once during the translation of the Book of Mormon, Joseph got frustrated with Emma and said something unkind to her. He tried translating soon after but he could not see anything to translate. He went to the nearby woods to repent to God for his mistake. Then he went immediately to apologize to Emma. The translation went smoothly for the rest of the day.

> JOSEPH BRIEFLY LOST THE ABILITY TO TRANSLATE UNTIL HE APOLOGIZED TO EMMA FOR UPSETTING HER.

261. During the period of translation, Joseph was shot at multiple times. He barely escaped with his life.

262. Mobs—usually led by other religious leaders—in Pennsylvania gathered together and persecuted Joseph and Oliver. Emma's father, Isaac Hale, became very friendly and kind to Joseph during this time, though, and he often defended Joseph from the mobs and persecutions.

Hale also allowed them to continue translating the Book of Mormon uninterrupted and protected while they lived in his home.

BAPTISMS OF JOSEPH SMITH AND OLIVER COWDERY

263. In May 1829, Joseph Smith was translating the record while Oliver Cowdery wrote exactly what Joseph dictated. Baptism was mentioned on the Urim and Thummim during translation, and they did not fully understand it at first. They went to the woods to pray about it, and a heavenly messenger appeared. It was John the Baptist, who baptized Jesus Christ.

264. John the Baptist laid his hands upon their heads and ordained them with the Aaronic Priesthood. He also told them that Joseph would be called to be the First Elder of the Church of Christ (as it was titled when first organized) and Oliver would be the Second.

265. John the Baptist then commanded Joseph to baptize Oliver and Oliver to baptize Joseph. The pair went to the Susquehanna River near Isaac Hale's home in Pennsylvania. Joseph baptized Oliver, and Oliver baptized Joseph. Technically, Oliver Cowdery was the first baptized member of the Church—not Joseph Smith!

266. Joseph Smith and Oliver Cowdery were baptized and given the Aaronic Priesthood on May 15, 1829.

267. The area on the Susquehanna River that Joseph owned, where the baptisms likely took place, is not usually very deep. It would not normally be deep enough for baptisms. However, in the year 1829, the river was overflowing from melted winter snow, making it deep enough for Joseph and Oliver to baptize each other correctly.

268. The Susquehanna River is the longest river on the east coast of the United States.

269. At first, Joseph and Oliver had to keep their baptisms a secret to avoid persecution while they were still translating the Book of Mormon.

270. Joseph disclosed that after he and Oliver were baptized, their minds were enlightened and they could understand the intention and true meaning of the messages of the scriptures.

271. The next person to be baptized into the Church was Joseph's younger brother Samuel Harrison Smith. He required a little bit of convincing of the truthfulness of the gospel at first. He prayed about it, and then he knew that what Joseph was saying was true. Oliver Cowdery baptized Samuel on May 25, 1829.

272. A few days after Samuel was baptized in Pennsylvania, he returned home to Palmyra. Hyrum heard about Samuel and Joseph's baptisms and desired to be baptized as well. He went to Pennsylvania to ask Joseph. Joseph inquired of the Lord, and Hyrum was also baptized.

273. Soon after the restoration of the Aaronic Priesthood, Joseph Smith and Oliver Cowdery were visited by three of Christ's Apostles: Peter, James, and John. They laid their hands on the heads of Joseph and Oliver and conferred them to the Melchizedek Priesthood.

274. The exact date of the restoration of the Melchizedek Priesthood was never recorded by Joseph or Oliver. According to Brigham Young, though, the Melchizedek Priesthood was also restored on the Susquehanna River, sometime between May 15 and June 18, 1829. By the time the Church was officially organized in 1830, both priesthoods had been restored to the earth.

275. Joseph and Oliver were not allowed by God to use their priesthood authority until after the Church was restored a year later.

Lucy Harris Sues Joseph Smith Jr.

276. After Martin Harris was prohibited from being Joseph's scribe any longer, his wife, Lucy Harris, tried prosecuting Joseph in a court of law in Lyons, New York. She claimed that he lied about having the gold plates and used that lie to manipulate Martin into giving him $200.

277. There were five total witnesses during this trial. Three witnesses, hired by Lucy Harris, did not know Joseph at all. The other two witnesses were Martin and Lucy Harris.

278. The first random witness claimed that Joseph once told him that the box that contained the plates did not hold gold plates at all. He asserted that Joseph told him that the box only held sand. The second witness declared that Joseph told him that the box was full of lead. The third witness accused Joseph of lying about anything being held in the box at all, that the box was empty!

279. Martin Harris was next to testify. He said to the judge, "I can swear that Joseph Smith never has got one dollar from me by persuasion, since God made me. I did once, on my own free will and accord, put $50 into his hands, in the presence of many witnesses, for the purpose of doing the work of the Lord. This, I can pointedly prove; and I can tell you, furthermore, that I have never seen in Joseph Smith a disposition to take any man's money without giving him reasonable compensation for the same in return. . . . He has the plates which he professes to have, if you do not believe it, but continue to resist the truth, it will one day be the means of damning your souls" (Lucy Mack Smith, *The History of Joseph Smith by His Mother*, 135). Martin Harris went against his own wife to testify of the truthfulness of what Joseph had claimed about the plates and the gospel.

> MARTIN HARRIS WENT AGAINST HIS OWN WIFE WHEN SHE SUED JOSEPH SMITH.

280. After hearing Martin Harris's testimony, the judge declared that he did not need to hear from any more witnesses. He tore up the case in front of everybody and then told them all to go home.

JOSEPH AND OLIVER MOVE TO WATERLOO

281. Joseph Smith Jr. and Oliver Cowdery faced so much persecution while translating the record in Harmony, Pennsylvania, that the mobs were even threatening to take their lives! The Lord commanded them to move to Waterloo, Ohio, into David Whitmer's home, to finish the translation. Joseph wrote David Whitmer a letter, requesting that he come pick them up from Pennsylvania and take them to his house in Waterloo to live and finish the translation.

282. Before Joseph Smith wrote to David Whitmer asking about moving in with him to translate the Book of Mormon, they had never met. Joseph only knew David's father, Peter Whitmer Sr.

283. About two years later, Oliver Cowdery married David Whitmer's sister—Elizabeth Ann.

284. When David Whitmer received the letter from the Prophet, he was unsure about going to pick them up. He spoke with his family about it. His father suggested that he try to get two days' worth of field work done in one day. If he could do that, he would have time to pick up Joseph and Oliver the following day, and Peter would take it as a sign from God that Joseph was telling the truth and that they needed to live with David to finish the Lord's work.

285. Whitmer succeeded in finishing two days' worth of work in one day, except for sowing plaster in the field. However, he woke up the next morning to find that the fields had been finished completely. Confused, David went to his sister's house nearby, and his sister told him that she and her children saw a few men sowing plaster in his fields early that morning. She assumed David hired them to finish his work so he could go to Joseph and Oliver, but David had not hired anybody. She told him that she had never seen anyone sowing plaster so quickly.

286. RUMOR: This has not been confirmed as fact; however, many Latter-day Saints believe that the random men sowing plaster in David Whitmer's fields that morning were the Three Nephites whom Christ blessed to continue dwelling on the earth, serving the Lord until He comes again. For Joseph Smith and Oliver Cowdery to finish the translation of the Book of Mormon safely, they needed to move into David Whitmer's home. That was God's plan. If sowing plaster in the field was the only thing keeping the translation of the Book of Mormon from being completed, it is possible that the Three Nephites made a trip to Waterloo to help. The story of the Three Nephites can be found in 3 Nephi 28 of the Book of Mormon.

287. David Whitmer went to Joseph Smith and Oliver Cowdery in Pennsylvania to bring them to his home. Joseph and Oliver moved to Waterloo, Ohio, for a short time. Emma stayed in Pennsylvania with her family during the completion of the translation.

288. To ensure the safety of the plates while he traveled to Waterloo, Joseph Smith gave the plates back to the angel Moroni until he arrived safely at David Whitmer's home.

289. David Whitmer insisted that Joseph and Oliver stay with him free of charge. He also arranged for his brother and himself to assist in translating whenever they were able.

290. Joseph Smith completed the translation of the Book of Mormon in only sixty-five working days. That means there were some days when they were not able to work on the translation while traveling or due to illness, but the sum of translation days would equal approximately sixty-five. That is a little over two months in translation days. It is difficult to even read the Book of Mormon that quickly.

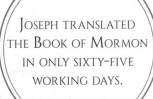

JOSEPH TRANSLATED THE BOOK OF MORMON IN ONLY SIXTY-FIVE WORKING DAYS.

291. The original manuscript of the Book of Mormon does not include any punctuation. This is evidence of the manuscript being a dictation—it suggests that Joseph read aloud the translation from the stones, and his scribes wrote it as he spoke.

292. No sections have been added or deleted from the original Book of Mormon manuscript. Most of the changes that have occurred were to fix punctuation and grammatical errors.

293. However, Joseph Smith removed about forty "and it came to pass" phrases. The use of the phrase is not very excessive in the King James Version of the Bible, but it is used very frequently in the original Hebrew version of the Bible. This is more evidence of the truthfulness of the Book of Mormon because the excessive use of the phrase was common during Biblical times.

294. Even the title page of the Book of Mormon was translated by Joseph Smith! It is a literal translation found on the left side of the very last page of the golden plates. Neither Joseph, his scribes, nor his publisher produced it. It was likely written anciently by either Mormon or Moroni.

PUBLISHING THE
BOOK OF MORMON

295.   Joseph Smith finished translating the record and sent for his parents
        to come read it immediately. Joseph's parents—and Martin Harris—
        came the day after receiving the message. They spent the entire evening
        reading the manuscript, completely realizing the full magnitude of the
        work Joseph was called to do in these latter days. They felt tremendous
        amounts of joy and peace.

296.   During the translation of the Book of Mormon, the Lord revealed that
        there were to be three witnesses to the Book of Mormon. They would
        see an angel, and they would see the plates. They would bear testimony
        of the Book of Mormon in writing for all generations to understand its
        truthfulness. Oliver Cowdery, David Whitmer, and Martin Harris all
        desired to be one of the three witnesses. They pleaded with Joseph to ask
        God if they could be chosen.

297.   The Smith family really loved Martin Harris, and Martin Harris really
        loved the Smith family. The morning after the Smiths and Martin
        Harris read the manuscript, Joseph came to Martin Harris and told
        him to humble himself and receive forgiveness of his sins from God.
        If Martin did so, he would be blessed in seeing the plates as one of the
        three witnesses, with Oliver Cowdery and David Whitmer.

298.   The three witnesses of the Book of Mormon are Oliver Cowdery,
        David Whitmer, and Martin Harris. The eight witnesses of the Book
        of Mormon are Christian Whitmer, Jacob Whitmer, Peter Whitmer
        Jr., John Whitmer, Joseph Smith Sr., Hyrum Smith, Samuel Harrison
        Smith, and Hiram Page.

299.   The revelation from Heavenly Father that reveals the men who
        were chosen to be the three witnesses can be found in Doctrine and
        Covenants 17.

300. Joseph and the three witnesses—Martin, Oliver, and David—went to the woods near the Whitmers' home and prayed earnestly. It required a lot of time, effort, and faith before their prayers were answered. An angel appeared and confirmed the truth about what Joseph had claimed regarding the golden plates.

301. At first, the four men were receiving no answers from God. Eventually, Martin Harris expressed that he believed his presence was keeping an angel from appearing to them. He left and went to another spot in the woods to pray alone. Initially, the angel only came to Joseph, Oliver, and David. After the angel left them, Joseph went to find Martin. Joseph prayed with Martin, who then beheld the same vision that the others had witnessed. It is believed that Martin Harris still had to repent a little more for his loss of the 116 pages or maybe for doubting his testimony before he could see the angel.

302. The angel showed the plates to Martin, Oliver, and David. The angel then turned each page, one by one, so the witnesses could distinctly see the engravings on the gold leaves.

303. After the angel departed, Joseph brought the plates to the eight witnesses. They also got to see each page and feel them too.

304. The statements signed by these eleven witnesses can be found after the introduction page of the Book of Mormon.

THE GOLD PLATES WERE GIVEN BACK TO THE ANGEL MORONI.

305. Right after the witnesses saw and held the plates, the angel Moroni came to Joseph. Joseph gave Moroni the plates so that nobody on earth could ever find them, violate them, change them, or destroy them.

306. That night, all the witnesses and their family members met at David Whitmer's home. They all bore testimony to one another and their family members about what they saw and heard.

307. The Book of Mormon was published in Palmyra, New York, in the print shop owned by Egbert Bratt (E. B.) Grandin.

308. At first, E. B. Grandin was hesitant to publish the Book of Mormon due to religious reasons and fear of persecution. Joseph went to Rochester, New York, and found another publisher who was willing to print the Book of Mormon. Before signing an official agreement, Joseph went

back to E. B. Grandin and asked him again to publish it. E. B. Grandin, with a little convincing from his associates, decided that he wanted to make a profit and that he would not be responsible for the book's contents just by being the printer.

309. Joseph Smith's agreement with E. B. Grandin was that Grandin would print 5,000 copies of the Book of Mormon for the price of $3,000.

310. At the time, publishers only printed a couple hundred copies of a book. To print 5,000 copies was unheard of. It was made possible through the brand new printing press equipment that E. B. Grandin had in his printing office.

311. Joseph and Hyrum paid for half of the payment to E. B. Grandin together and Martin Harris paid the other half himself.

312. Joseph received the revelation from God that while the Book of Mormon was being printed, Oliver needed to transcribe the whole manuscript over again so they always had an extra copy just in case. The Lord also told Joseph that he should only bring one page of the manuscript to the printing office at a time and always have a guard with him. The guard needed to keep watch over the Smith house night and day to protect the manuscript as well.

JOSEPH ONLY GAVE THE PRINTING PRESS ONE PAGE OF THE MANUSCRIPT AT A TIME.

313. For safety against the mobs in Palmyra, Joseph received promptings to move himself and his family to Waterloo, Ohio, while the Book of Mormon was being printed. Joseph Smith Sr. also went to Waterloo with Joseph and Emma, as God had told him to do so. Hyrum moved to Colesville for a short time.

314. Lucy kept the manuscript at her house inside the chest, which was locked and placed under the head of her bed. There was always a guard outside the Smith house for protection too.

315. Oliver Cowdery once overheard an angry conversation from a group that had rallied together to express their fears about the publishing of the Book of Mormon. They knew it would probably ruin everything they believed and it would discredit their ministers and religious leaders. They concluded that they would send three men to the Smith home. The men would try to trick Lucy into reading the manuscript to

them, distract her, steal the entire manuscript, and throw it in a fire. Each member of the group vowed to never purchase a single copy of the Book of Mormon and to forbid any of their family members to purchase or read it.

316. Oliver Cowdery immediately went to Lucy to tell her about the angry group's plans. Lucy was not at all afraid or worried. She said that she would not take out the manuscript to read it to them unless she chose to do so, and the men would not be able to do anything about it.

317. Lucy Mack Smith was short in stature, but many people who knew her described her as "small but mighty." When the designated three men from the group came to the Smith home and asked Lucy to read the manuscript to them, she refused several times. They realized they were not going to succeed in stealing the manuscript. Instead, they asked her to at least stop talking about the Book of Mormon around town and to have her kids stop talking about it too. She replied, "If you should stick my flesh full of faggots (small pieces of wood used as fuel to a fire), and even burn me at the stake, I would declare as long as God should give me breath, that Joseph has got that Record, and that I know it to be true" (Lucy Mack Smith, *The History of Joseph Smith by His Mother*, 150). The Prophet's mother sure was "small but mighty!"

318. The same group who tried stealing the manuscript from Lucy went to E. B. Grandin and tried convincing him of the evil consequences of printing the Book of Mormon. Grandin halted the printing process because he was afraid of the repercussions. Joseph Smith had to return to Palmyra for a short time to reassure him. Then he started printing the Book of Mormon again.

319. A separate mob of about forty men gathered together with a plan to beat up the Prophet while he was on his way to the printing office with a page of the manuscript. Lucy heard about this and was really worried for her son's safety. Joseph comforted her and said that nothing would hurt him that day. On his way to the printing office, he found the mob lined up, each sitting on top of a farm fence on the right side of the road that Joseph traveled on. Joseph walked up to each of them one by one, tipped his hat, and said, "Good morning." The mob members sat there speechless, on the fence, in total confusion. Before they knew it, Joseph was long gone. The only choice they had was to just return to their homes.

320. During the printing process, a new paper was established in Palmyra called *The Reflector*. "The Dogberry Papers" were articles that illegally published portions of the Book of Mormon weekly in *The Reflector* newspaper. The excerpts were also combined with lies and slander.

321. Joseph Smith went to the E. B. Grandin's printing shop where Esquire Cole (the author of the articles) was stealing pages of the Book of Mormon to publish in his paper. Joseph spoke with Cole on the matter, telling him he needed to stop publishing the Book of Mormon without Joseph's permission. Joseph owned the copyright and therefore could prosecute Esquire Cole for copyright infringement. Esquire Cole then stopped illegally publishing portions of the Book of Mormon.

322. The Book of Mormon finished publication in March 1830. The Church of Jesus Christ of Latter-day Saints was officially organized one month later.

323. There are several passages in the Holy Bible that prophesied of the coming forth of the Book of Mormon. One of the most famous passages is Ezekiel 37, which prophesies of two books being brought forth as testaments of Jesus Christ. They are the Bible and the Book of Mormon.

324. Years later, Joseph Smith hid the original manuscript of the Book of Mormon in the cornerstone of the Nauvoo House. The protective lead box that contained them had been broken, and the manuscript had received lots of water damage. Most of it was worn down or lost.

ORGANIZATION AND EARLY YEARS OF THE CHURCH

325.   The very first meeting of The Church of Jesus Christ of Latter-day Saints was held on April 6, 1830, at Peter Whitmer Sr.'s farm.

326.   The Church of Jesus Christ of Latter-day Saints was organized on April 6, 1830. Oddly, that day was a Tuesday, not a Sunday. The Lord commanded Joseph Smith to hold the first meeting on this day specifically. It has been confirmed by revelation and several apostles and prophets that April 6 is the actual and accurate date of the birth of Christ. This could be why Heavenly Father wanted Christ's Church restored on this date.

> THE CHURCH OF JESUS CHRIST OF LATTER-DAY SAINTS WAS OFFICIALLY ORGANIZED ON A TUESDAY, NOT A SUNDAY.

327.   Some speculate that the Church was actually organized in the Smith home in Manchester, New York. However, both Joseph Smith and David Whitmer were very clear in their records about the location of the organization of the Church at Peter Whitmer Sr.'s farm.

328.   In 1830, the name of the Church was simply "The Church of the Latter-day Saints."

329.   Only six official Church members attended the very first meeting at Whitmer Farm in 1830. These six members were Joseph Smith, Oliver Cowdery, Samuel Harrison Smith, Hyrum Smith, David Whitmer, and Peter Whitmer Sr.

330.   To legally start an official church in 1830, Joseph Smith only needed six official members. However, there were several friends and family members also invited to the first Church meeting.

331. Some of those in attendance at the meeting were baptized that same day. They were: Joseph Smith Sr., Lucy Mack Smith, Martin Harris, and Orrin Porter Rockwell. When his father was baptized, Joseph wept tears of pure joy!

332. Newel Knight was an active early member of the Church. In the first few months of the Church's official organization, he decided he wanted to pray vocally at the next meeting. He was too afraid and claimed he would rather pray by himself. Newel went to the woods the next day to pray but found it to be extremely difficult. He felt physically awful, like evil was surrounding him. He returned home, unable to pray. His wife noticed he looked different and was acting strange. He did not seem in control of his own body. It frightened her so much that she sent for Joseph to come see Newel.

333. By the time Joseph arrived at Newel's home, there were almost ten other people there who had heard loud noises coming from the house. Joseph grabbed Newel's hand, and Newel immediately implored Joseph to cast the devil out of him. Joseph said that if Newel had faith, then Joseph could do so. Joseph rebuked and commanded the devil to leave in the name of Jesus Christ. Newel Knight declared that he physically saw the devil leave his body and then vanish. Joseph Smith wrote that this was the first miracle performed in the restored Church of Jesus Christ.

334. Many of the neighbors came to Newel Knight's house that night and witnessed Joseph casting out evil. Because of what they saw, they believed that Joseph was a true prophet and they became members of the Church.

335. The first ever general conference was held on June 9, 1830. There were twenty-seven people in attendance. Back then, they just called it "conference." The term "general conference" usually meant a regional meeting back then. However, by 1839, the term "general conference" referred to semi-annual conferences where business was conducted with the whole Church, like the general conferences we hold today.

THE FIRST GENERAL CONFERENCE WAS HELD ON JUNE 9, 1830.

336. Emma Hale Smith was among those baptized on the day of the first general conference. However, she was not confirmed until one month

later because the Prophet was arrested for teaching the Book of Mormon and angering non-Mormons in the area.

337. The constable was actually working with a mob who desired to beat, tar and feather, and run the Prophet out on a rail (a popular punishment in the 1800s where a mob would force their victim—who was usually also tarred and feathered—to straddle a wooden pole, carried on both ends by the mob, to the outskirts of town and leave them there). The original plan was that the constable would meet the mob in the previously designated location where the mob would take Joseph and cause harm. Once the constable actually met Joseph, though, he believed that the Prophet was a good man. Instead, he saved Joseph from the attacks of the mob by speeding away with Joseph in his horse-drawn carriage. The constable let Joseph stay at his house that night. He even slept by the door holding a gun to make sure nobody could get in to harm the Prophet.

338. Since there was a warrant for Joseph's arrest, he was still sent to trial. He was defended by two men, who were not lawyers and did not have training in law. According to Joseph, they were filled with the power of God. They were able to get Joseph Smith acquitted. Even those who were convinced of Joseph's guilt in these crimes before the trial began realized the accusations were not true. Some even came to apologize to the Prophet afterward and warn him of the mobs waiting outside the court to attack him. One of these men led Joseph back to the Prophet's home safely through a private route.

339. In July 1830, when Oliver Cowdery was living with Peter Whitmer Sr., Oliver wrote Joseph a letter claiming there was an error in the Book of Commandments section 2 paragraph 7 (Doctrine and Covenants 20:37). He declared it was completely false and demanded Joseph erase the paragraph. Joseph immediately wrote back to him asking by what authority Oliver took upon himself to order Joseph to change one of God's commandments. Joseph went to Peter Whitmer Sr.'s house to visit Oliver and the rest of the family.

340. The Whitmers all seemed to agree with Oliver Cowdery that the paragraph in Book of Commandments was incorrect. Joseph continually tried speaking with them calmly as the others were getting heated in their discussion. Eventually, Christian Whitmer agreed with Joseph and helped him speak to the family and Oliver. Cowdery and the Whitmer family finally agreed that they were in error before. Joseph Smith often

used this story as a lesson in being humble and meek so the Lord can teach us.

341. In July 1830, Joseph received a revelation from God regarding his wife Emma. It can be found today in Doctrine and Covenants 25. Emma Smith is an "elect lady" called by Heavenly Father to be a comforter and supporter of Joseph Smith. She is called to be a scribe when Oliver is gone and to select the songs for the hymnbook. Most of the songs she chose are still in the hymnbooks used today.

342. During the 1830s, most people traveling long distances avoided traveling on foot. They journeyed mostly by horse or carriage. The first LDS missionaries, who ventured from New York to Ohio, only traveled on foot through villages and towns so they could speak with people and spread the gospel easier. Being a missionary has always been hard work!

343. In August 1830, the Lord commanded Joseph and Hyrum Smith and John and David Whitmer to visit the Church in Colesville, New York. Since mob violence and persecution was worsening in the area, it was not a good time for these men to travel anywhere. The Lord commanded them to go, so they knew they had to do it. The men prayed that they would be safe on their journey. God answered their prayers. Several times during their trip, they passed some of their enemies who stared at them but did not recognize them! They traveled completely unharmed. They arrived in Colesville that night and held a joyful meeting where they confirmed several members, bore testimony, and partook of the sacrament.

344. In August 1830, Joseph Smith was again living in Harmony, Pennsylvania, with Emma's family. A Methodist minister, who was one of the leaders of the persecution of the Prophet, knew Emma's father was protecting Joseph from the mobs. The minister visited Isaac Hale's home and accused Joseph of many evil things. They were all lies to convince Emma's family to stop believing in and protecting the Prophet. Unfortunately, it worked. The entire Hale family turned against Joseph Smith.

PARLEY P. PRATT READ THE ENTIRE BOOK OF MORMON IN ONE NIGHT.

345. A man named Parley P. Pratt read the entire Book of Mormon in one night! He immediately was convinced of its truth. He

traveled to Palmyra to meet Hyrum Smith and was baptized by Oliver Cowdery in September 1830.

346. In September 1830, a man named Hiram Page found a stone and claimed to receive two revelations from it regarding the future of the Church and its members. His "revelations" deceived many, even the Whitmers and Oliver Cowdery. However, Joseph Smith and other members of the Church enquired of the Lord. Joseph received the revelation found in Doctrine and Covenants section 28. The revelation states that no members of the Church receive revelation for the entire Church except those in authority to do so, specifically the prophet. The Lord explained that we receive revelation for what we have stewardship over; bishops receive revelation for their ward, Relief Society presidents can receive revelation about their ward Relief Society, parents can receive revelation about their families, and we receive revelation about ourselves.

347. Once Joseph Smith explained this revelation to the Church, Hiram Page and all those whom he deceived renounced the false revelations from the stone and knew the Prophet Joseph Smith was the only one who could receive revelation for the whole Church at that time. Joseph Smith never told Hiram that his visions never occurred, only that they were not of God and that Hiram himself was deceived by them.

348. Shortly after arriving in Kirtland, on May 1, 1831, Emma gave birth prematurely to a pair of twins who both died almost immediately. That same day, another pair of twins was born in Kirtland. Their mother died in labor. The father offered to give the orphan twins to Emma and Joseph. They adopted the twins and raised them as their own. They were Julia Murdock Smith and Joseph Murdock Smith. Joseph Murdock Smith died as an infant.

349. At a conference held June 3–6, 1831, some elders were ordained to the office of the High Priesthood (Melchezidek Priesthood) for the very first time since Christ and His Apostles. They were ordained by Joseph Smith. According to their records, it was one of the most spiritual conferences they had.

350. In July 1831, Joseph Smith visited Independence, Missouri, Jackson County, where God manifested Himself to the Prophet and revealed Independence to be the gathering spot of Zion (the New Jerusalem).

351. After being converted to the restored gospel, Sidney Rigdon and his wife and children were kicked out of their home because it was built for

them by their previous church. They lost their house and their livelihood to join the true Church.

352. In November 1831, the Book of Commandments (Doctrine and Covenants) was being printed at the Church's printing press in Independence, Missouri. The press was established by William W. Phelps. The plan was to print 10,000 copies, but due to difficulties, only 3,000 copies were initially printed.

353. William E. McLellin once prayed in secret that the Lord would tell Joseph the answers to all five of William's specific spiritual questions. Without telling the Prophet what his questions actually were, William requested Joseph to ask God to answer his questions through the Prophet. Joseph returned with every answer to each of William's concerns. The Lord made both the questions and the answers known to Joseph through revelation. God's answers to McLellin's questions can be found in Doctrine and Covenants 66.

354. In the year 1832, Joseph Smith prophesied of an upcoming war between the northern and southern states in the United States of America. This revelation from God can be found in Doctrine and Covenants 87. The Civil War began April 1861, nearly thirty years after the Lord revealed it to Joseph. By the time the Civil War commenced, Joseph Smith had been dead for almost twenty years.

JOSEPH PROPHESIED THE CIVIL WAR NEARLY THIRTY YEARS BEFORE IT BEGAN.

355. Joseph Smith was ordained as President of the High Priesthood on January 25, 1832. He was sustained to this calling on April 26, 1832.

356. The original First Presidency of the Church had Joseph Smith Jr. as President, with Jesse Gause and Sidney Rigdon as his counselors. Unfortunately, Jesse Gause was eventually excommunicated.

357. In November 1832, Brigham Young and his brother visited the Prophet's home in Kirtland. Brigham spoke to Joseph in tongues, in the perfect Adamic language. The perfect Adamic language was the language spoken by Adam and Eve and the language that we believe is spoken in heaven. Joseph later wrote that he knew at that moment that Brigham Young would one day lead the Church. Many believe Brigham Young said this to Joseph while speaking in tongues, but the record is unclear.

358. In December 1832, the Lord revealed to Joseph Smith a commandment to build a holy temple in Kirtland.

JOSEPH SMITH TRANSLATION OF THE BIBLE

359. In September 1831, Joseph and Emma moved to Hiram, Ohio, to translate the incorrect portions of the Holy Bible. They lived with John Johnson on his farm. Sidney Rigdon lived nearby and was Joseph's scribe for the Bible translation.

360. Joseph fixed and added portions of the King James Version of the Bible that had been lost or changed. We have access to it now in the footnotes of the LDS King James Version of the Bible. Along with the Book of Mormon and other scriptures, it is part of the fulness of Christ's gospel that Joseph Smith restored, after it was lost or changed in the thousands of years following Christ's death.

361. While Joseph Smith translated the Bible, he did not need the Urim and Thummim for translation anymore because he was so well acquainted with the spirit of revelation. He could translate without using them.

362. Many assume that it took Joseph Smith the entire rest of his life to complete the Bible translation because it was not yet published at the time of his death. However, the Joseph Smith Translation of the Bible took three years to complete. He started only three months after publishing the Book of Mormon in 1830.

363. Joseph Smith completed the translation of the King James Bible in July 1833.

364. While translating the Bible, Joseph and his family lived with John and Elsa Johnson on their farm. Before meeting the Prophet, Elsa Johnson had a handicap in one of her arms which caused her crippling pain and limited her movements. Joseph Smith gave her a blessing and she was immediately healed. She never had any problems with her arm again. She and her husband were converted to the gospel because of this.

365. On February 16, 1832, Joseph Smith was translating the Bible with Sidney Rigdon as his scribe in the home of John Johnson. While they were translating, Joseph and Sidney saw a vision of the plan of salvation.

366. They witnessed the celestial kingdom, terrestrial kingdom, telestial kingdom, and outer darkness. The revelation is found in Doctrine and Covenants 76. Joseph said of this vision, "Nothing could be more pleasing to the saint, upon the order of the kingdom of the Lord, than the light which burst upon the world through the foregoing vision. Every law, every commandment, every promise, every truth, and every point, touching to the destiny of man, from Genesis to Revelation, where the purity of either remains unsullied from the wisdom of men, goes to [show] the perfection of the theory, and witness the fact that that document is a transcript from the Records of the eternal world. . . . The rewards for faithfulness and punishment for sins, are so much beyond the narrowmindedness of men, that every honest man is constrained to exclaim: *It came from God*" (Joseph Smith, in *History of the Church*, 1:198).

367. After the Prophet's death, the original manuscript of the Joseph Smith Translation of the Bible was in the possession of Emma. She gave it to The Re-Organized Church of Jesus Christ of Latter-day Saints (now referred to as the Community of Christ).

368. The Community of Christ published it as the "New Translation." The Church of Jesus Christ of Latter-day Saints was unsure about the "New Translation" because they did not know if the Community of Christ had changed any of its contents from the original manuscript. Eventually, LDS Church historians were given permission to review the original manuscript and discovered that there were no major changes made between it and the "New Translation." The changes that Joseph originally added to the Bible are now available to The Church of Jesus Christ of Latter-day Saints as well.

369. John Johnson's son, Olmsted Johnson, came home to visit his family at the farm on February 22, 1832. Olmsted had apostatized from the Church. Joseph told him that if he did not obey the gospel teachings, he would never return to see his father again. Olmsted did not believe Joseph and therefore did not heed the Prophet's warning. Shortly after, he went to the southern states and was too sick to return home. He died in Virginia soon after.

370. Joseph Smith and John Johnson share a common ancient relative. The relative is Joseph of Egypt, from the Old Testament of the Bible.

Tarring and Feathering at Johnson Farm

371. On March 25, 1832, in Hiram, Ohio, Joseph and Emma Smith's adopted twins were sick. Joseph was sleeping on the trundle bed (pull-out bed underneath an actual bed) in his room while Emma was sleeping in the bed above with one of the sick twins.

372. Phoebe and Sidney Rigdon, who lived nearby, had children who were also sick with the same illness that night.

373. Emma was half asleep, half awake. She heard light tapping on the window next to her bed. She assumed it was the wind or tree branches. What Emma did not realize was that an angry mob was outside the house, tapping the window to see if Joseph and Emma were asleep.

> EMMA SMITH WAS PREGNANT WITH THEIR SON JOSEPH SMITH III WHEN THE MOB CAME.

374. Emma was pregnant with their son Joseph Smith III.

375. All of a sudden, Joseph was awakened by his wife's piercingly loud, frantic screaming. He then realized Emma was screaming because he was being violently carried out of his bed by a dozen men. Some grabbed his arms and legs, some had his hair, some held Joseph by his clothing.

376. Joseph freed one of his legs and forcefully kicked the face of the man who initially held it. It made the man bleed from his nose. This really angered the mob, who threatened to kill Joseph if he kept fighting back. Joseph had no choice but to let them attack him and beat him.

377. Some men in the mob grabbed Joseph by the neck and choked him until he passed out. He was unconscious for a little while.

378. When the Prophet regained consciousness, he noticed that his good friend and scribe for the translation of the Bible, Sidney Rigdon, was lying unconscious, tarred and feathered, on the ground. The mob had dragged Rigdon from his home by his heels. Joseph thought the mob must have murdered Sidney. The Prophet then began to plead for his own life.

379. Joseph was a decently large and strong man. They did not want to risk Joseph getting his feet underneath himself to fight back and run away.

The mob never let go of Joseph or ever let any part of his body even touch the ground.

380. Joseph had to listen in fear while the mob held him, discussing whether they should kill the Prophet or not. The mob was very divided on the matter, but eventually they decided not to kill him but instead beat him, strip his clothes off, and tar and feather him.

381. The men tore off all the Prophet's clothing.

382. The mob tried to force a vial of poison into the Prophet's mouth, but he physically refused to open his mouth. Joseph then broke the vial with his teeth. When he did so, he also chipped his tooth. The chip in his tooth caused the Prophet to have a slight whistle whenever he spoke for the rest of his life.

383. Since Joseph broke the vial of poison, the mob instead tried forcing the paddle of hot tar in his mouth. Joseph defended himself by keeping his mouth closed and moving his head around so they could not succeed in getting tar inside his mouth. The mob did cover his mouth and nose with tar though, so the Prophet could not breathe.

384. Joseph believed the leader of the mob was a man named Symonds Ryder who seemed to be delegating responsibilities to the other mob members. Symonds Ryder turned against the Prophet when Joseph once misspelled Ryder's name as "Simonds Rider." He supposed that must mean that Joseph Smith was a liar and not a prophet of God and he left the Church.

385. Symonds Ryder went on to be influential in the foundation of the Disciples Church. Ironically, on his tombstone, "Disciples" is misspelled as "Deciple." There's nothing "Simonds Rider" can do about it now. Whoever said God does not have a sense of humor?

386. The mob left Joseph alone on the ground, beaten, exposed, covered in hot tar and feathers, and unable to breathe. He tried to stand up but fell down again because he was too weak. He had to pull the sticky, hot tar from his mouth and nose to breathe before he had the strength to stand up and walk home.

387. Joseph spoke about how he felt like his spirit left his body and then watched the mob attack him, like an out-of-body experience.

388. When Joseph finally stumbled to John Johnson's front door, the tar he was covered in looked, to Emma, like blood. She thought he was

beaten so badly to be bleeding from every part of his body. The pregnant Emma fainted from stress and shock at the sight of her husband.

389. The LDS sisters in the neighborhood heard the commotion and came to Joseph and Emma's aid. They gathered in Joseph and Emma's room until the Prophet returned home. Since Emma was unconscious and Joseph had no clothes, the sisters quickly tossed the Prophet a blanket at his request to cover himself, and then they shut the door until Joseph was ready to walk inside. Emma, the Johnsons, and the Church members in the neighborhood spent the entire rest of the night helping get the tacky tar off Joseph's body—scraping, washing, cleaning—so he could wear clothes again to speak in the Church meeting the next morning.

390. The feathers that the mob covered Joseph with were stolen from Sidney Rigdon and his wife's pillows after Sidney was dragged out of his home. One of the mob men returned, attempting to get more feathers, but the neighborhood women locked him inside the house until the rest of the mob left.

> THE FEATHERS THAT THE MOB USED WERE STOLEN FROM SIDNEY RIGDON'S PILLOWS.

391. Some members of the mob from the night before—including Symonds Ryder—were in the congregation that day, attempting to either taunt Joseph or see if he would have the strength and courage to speak. Joseph was not afraid of them.

392. Most of the mobbers had family members who believed Joseph Smith, and they kept their violent actions a secret from their faithful families.

393. Despite Joseph's face and body being scratched, burned, and painful, he still preached like normal and even baptized three people after the meeting.

394. Joseph had been persecuted a lot, but the persecutors had never been violent until that night when Joseph and Sidney were tarred and feathered. It was shocking and devastating to the Prophet, his family, Rigdon's family, and the members of the Church.

395. Joseph Murdock Smith was the sick infant that was lying in bed with Emma the night Joseph was tarred and feathered. He had a cold that worsened from exposure to the chill outside after the mob kidnapped his adoptive father. He died five days later, on March 30, 1832.

396.   Joseph went to visit Sidney Rigdon on the day following the tarring and feathering. Sidney Rigdon survived the mob attack but had sustained a major head injury. Joseph said that Sidney was acting very strange. His head was highly inflamed from being dragged out by his heels and unable to lift his head off the ground. Joseph believed that Sidney was never the same person after his head injury.

397.   Sidney Rigdon had the strong opinion that he was supposed to be the next prophet after Joseph Smith died, but many scholars and historians suppose that Rigdon might have been incapable of doing so after his injury. God planned to have Brigham Young succeed Joseph Smith. Joseph Smith even once said, "Brother Sidney [Rigdon] is a man whom I love, but is not capable of that pure and steadfast love for those who are his benefactors that should possess the breast of a president of the Church of Christ. This with some other little things such as selfishness, and independence of mind, which, too often manifested, destroys the confidence of those who would lay down their lives for him: but notwithstanding these things he is a great and good man, a man of great power of words, and can gain the friendship of his hearers very quick. He is a man whom God will uphold, if he will continue faithful to his calling. O God, grant that he may, for the Lord's Sake, Amen" (Joseph Smith, in *History of the Church*, 1:208).

398.   For the rest of Joseph's life, he had to comb his hair in a way that covered his permanent bald spot caused by the burning tar.

> JOSEPH HAD A PERMANENT BALD SPOT ON HIS HEAD FROM THE BURNING TAR.

399.   Joseph and Emma continued to live with the Johnsons for a while after the tarring and feathering. Sidney Rigdon moved away to Kirtland, Ohio.

KIRTLAND, OHIO

400. There were more revelations given to Joseph Smith in Kirtland and surrounding areas than in any other location during the Prophet's lifetime.

401. Joseph Smith III was born on November 6, 1832, while his father, Joseph Smith, was on a mission in the east. Joseph Smith III became the President of The Re-Organized Church of Jesus Christ of Latter-day Saints (now Community of Christ) in 1860.

402. At one of the first conferences held in Kirtland, Joseph told the Saints they had no idea the destiny of the Church and of God's kingdom. He prophesied that the Saints would travel to the Rocky Mountains and build temples. This prophecy was fulfilled when the prophet Brigham Young led the Saints to Salt Lake City after Joseph's death.

403. Newspapers in Kirtland were not sure what to call the Saints, since they did not have an official name for themselves yet. Some called the Saints "Josephites," "Gold Biblers," etc. A newspaper editor named Eber D. Howe was notorious for making up nicknames to describe different subjects in his newspapers. He called the Saints "the Mormonites." Other newspapers caught on and everybody called them "Mormonites," and the name eventually became simply "the Mormons." This was the first use of the term "Mormons." It was not a very affectionate nickname for the Latter-day Saints at the time.

404. In the summer of 1832, Joseph and Newel K. Whitney were coming back from Missouri to Kirtland. The horses carrying their carriage were spooked and started running at dangerous speed. Joseph jumped out of the carriage unharmed, but Newel's leg got stuck on one of the wheels. It broke his leg. Joseph stayed behind with his friend to help take care of him for a couple weeks.

405. Newel and Joseph stayed at a public house. Public houses were big houses that doubled as inns or hotels. While he was staying at a public house in Greenville, Joseph's food was poisoned. The poison made him so violently ill that he dislocated his jaw while vomiting. Joseph popped his own jaw back into place with his hands, which must have been painful. He ran to Newel Whitney and told him it was not safe and they needed to leave immediately. The Prophet gave Newel a blessing and his leg was healed instantly. They traveled home to Kirtland safely.

406. On February 9, 1834, Martin Harris was taken to Church disciplinary court because he told somebody that Joseph Smith drank too much alcohol before and while translating the Book of Mormon. He confessed and stated that he was trying to make the Church look bad. He was remorseful and was forgiven. This is one of the stories easily misconstrued by some people today, but it is important to note that Martin Harris himself admitted that his claims were wrong.

407. At a conference on May 3, 1834, the Prophet and the Twelve prayerfully decided to name the Church "The Church of Jesus Christ of Latter-day Saints" (or simply "The Church of the Latter-day Saints").

408. In 1836, there were about 1,500–2,000 members of the Church, just in the Kirtland branch.

409. In January 1836, a Connecticut minister named John W. Olived visited Joseph Smith's home. He asked Joseph several questions about the beliefs of the Church. He asked how the Saints differ from other religions. Joseph replied saying that other religions do not believe the Bible, but we do. The minister claimed he believed the Bible, and Joseph replied by telling him to get baptized. The minister declined but continued to ask questions. He was amazed and astonished by the Prophet's answers.

JOSEPH ONCE WORE WOMEN'S CLOTHING TO ESCAPE THE MOBS.

410. Joseph once had to wear women's clothing to escape Kirtland undetected by the mobs.

SCHOOL OF PROPHETS

411. After returning from a mission to the eastern United States, Joseph Smith established the School of Prophets in one of the rooms on the second floor of the Newel K. Whitney store, where he and his family lived at the time.

412. The School of Prophets functioned as both an academic school for the brethren as well as sort of an early and unofficial elders quorum.

413. There were countless amazing visions and commandments revealed in the School of Prophets, including the Word of Wisdom.

414. William McLellin, who was a schoolteacher, wrote that he had taught school in five different states but had never seen students make more rapid progress than those of the School of Prophets.

415. Lucy Mack Smith once visited the School of Prophets and wrote that she felt the Spirit there so strongly that she thought the members of the Church would have eternal peace and no longer experience pain and suffering.

416. On February 14, 1835, Joseph Smith asked the three witnesses of the Book of Mormon (Martin Harris, David Whitmer, and Oliver Cowdery) to pray about it together, and then they chose the first Quorum of the Twelve Apostles of the restored Church. They chose (in order) Lyman E. Johnson, Brigham Young, Heber C. Kimball, Orson Hyde, David W. Patten, Luke Johnson, William E. McLellin, John C. Boynton, Orson Pratt, William Smith, Thomas B. Marsh, and Parley P. Pratt.

417. Ten of the Twelve were ordained to their offices on either February 14 or 15, 1835. Orson Pratt and Thomas B. Marsh, however, were not ordained until April because they were on missions when they were called.

418. The School of Prophets temporarily closed in March 1835, while the Quorum of the Twelve left on missions to spread the gospel.

Word of Wisdom

419. In the 1830s, the use of alcohol and tobacco was extremely excessive. Alcohol was used medically as a medication or an anesthetic during procedures. It was legally consumed by men, women, and even children, sometimes at every meal! It was consumed socially, and sometimes it was considered rude or weird to refuse it. Tobacco usage was almost just as common as the alcohol consumption of the time.

420. The brethren frequently chewed tobacco at their meetings in the School of Prophets. They did not have modern trashcans for the disposal of it, but instead used a metal can-like object. It had a funnel structure at the top and was rounded like a ball at the bottom. Men would often try spitting their chewing tobacco across the room into the can, and they rarely made it in.

421. Brigham Young claims he remembered Emma Smith cleaning up after them and feeling that the uncleanliness—tacky, sticky tobacco on the floor of such a special, spiritual setting—could not possibly bring the Holy Spirit into their meetings. She asked Joseph to inquire of the Lord about it. The Lord revealed to Joseph Smith the revelation found in Doctrine and Covenants 89, also known as the Word of Wisdom. The Word of Wisdom revealed that the consumption of alcohol, tobacco, and some other things was harmful to the body.

EMMA SMITH ASKED JOSEPH TO ASK THE LORD ABOUT TOBACCO, WHICH EVENTUALLY LED TO THE REVELATION KNOWN AS THE WORD OF WISDOM.

422. Joseph Smith first revealed the new revelation to some of the brethren in the School of Prophets. Some were smoking pipes. As soon as they heard Joseph tell them how the Lord desired that they stop, they all threw their pipes in the fire!

423. Because tobacco and alcohol were so common, the revelation of the Word of Wisdom was difficult for the Saints. They were accustomed to drinking alcohol and chewing tobacco all day, every day. It was a tough habit for them to break, and some of the Saints even refused to quit.

424. During the time when Joseph Smith led the Church, he interpreted the revelation to mean that these harmful substances and activities could

be used in moderation. During Joseph Smith's lifetime, the Word of Wisdom was more of a guideline than a requirement.

425. Years later, severe sickness struck the Saints in early Nauvoo. One of the sisters begged Joseph to allow hot tea to alleviate the illness symptoms. Joseph felt so bad for his sick friends. He said that if they only used the hot tea to help themselves feel better, they could partake of it in moderation. This same sister later wrote that this instance was the beginning of the Saints disobeying the Word of Wisdom and not taking it seriously.

426. It was not until the Saints settled in Utah that President Brigham Young commanded the Saints to use only water for the sacrament. He also commanded that abstinence, not moderation, was the correct way to live the Word of Wisdom.

CONSTRUCTION OF THE KIRTLAND TEMPLE

427. In December 1832, the Lord revealed to Joseph Smith a commandment for the Church to build a temple, a House of the Lord, in Kirtland. During construction, the Saints more often referred to the Kirtland Temple as "the House of the Lord," or just "the Meeting House."

428. Technically, God told Joseph Smith to have the Missouri Saints build a temple in Far West first. When the Missouri saints took too long to even get started, the Lord revealed that Joseph and the Kirtland Saints should build a temple in Ohio.

429. Before construction began, Joseph and a few other Saints saw the Kirtland Temple in heavenly visions.

430. The Lord even revealed the exact dimensions He wanted the temple to be. It was to be fifty-five feet wide and sixty-five feet long.

431. Joseph Smith was one day walking with some of the brethren to the spot where the Kirtland Temple would be built. He asked them if they knew anybody, any architects, who could design and construct the Kirtland House of the Lord (as they referred it back then). One of them suggested a non-Mormon friend named Artemus Millet, who lived in Canada. Joseph told Brigham Young to go on a mission to Canada, convert and

baptize Artemus Millet, and come back with Millet, Millet's family, and $1000. Brigham Young did exactly as the Prophet asked. Artemus Millet sold his Canadian farm, moved himself and his family to Kirtland, and oversaw the construction of the Kirtland House of the Lord from beginning to end.

432. Several Saints imagined the Kirtland Temple to be like a small log home. Joseph Smith declared at a meeting that they were not going to build a house for God with logs. The Lord told Joseph that He wanted the best and finest the Saints could produce. It was not a house for man; it was the house of the Lord. Joseph then laid out the full pattern and design of the temple. It made the Saints extraordinarily excited to build the House of the Lord.

> JOSEPH SENT BRIGHAM YOUNG TO CANADA TO CONVERT ARTEMUS MILLET AND BRING HIM BACK TO OVERSEE THE CONSTRUCTION OF THE KIRTLAND TEMPLE.

433. Artemus Millet brought a brand new and unusual Canadian building technique to the construction of the Temple. He did not build the Kirtland Temple using the common logs or bricks. Millet used large chunks of sandstone and then painted over them to make the House look beautiful. The Kirtland Temple stood out from other Ohio buildings because of its beauty and its unique, magnificent structure.

434. On June 5, 1833, George A. Smith drew the first load of stones for the Kirtland Temple.

435. The carpentry work of the Kirtland Temple was done mostly by Brigham Young.

436. Construction of the Kirtland Temple began in June 1833, at a time when the poverty level of the Saints was very high. Building the temple required a lot of sacrifice from the members of the Church.

437. Hyrum Smith dug a trench in the place where the Kirtland Temple was to be built on the first day of construction. He declared he wanted to be the first to strike a blow on the Lord's House.

438. Originally, the plan was to build three smaller temples in Kirtland. Instead, the Saints built one large temple. In comparison to the temples built by the Latter-day Saints in the years since, though, the Kirtland Temple is modest in size.

439. Constant threats of destruction to the Kirtland Temple forced the Saints to have guards on steady watch of the temple day and night.

440. Work on the temple slowed significantly in 1834 because many of the brethren went to aid the Missouri Saints with Zion's Camp.

441. The Kirtland Temple construction was completed soon after Joseph Smith returned from Zion's Camp in 1836.

ZION'S CAMP

442. One day, a messenger came to Joseph in Kirtland and told him that the Saints in Missouri were being wrongfully thrown in jail, beaten, tarred and feathered, and some were even murdered. Joseph's heart broke. He knew he needed to help the Missouri Saints.

443. "The Evening and Morning Star" was a newspaper series published by the Church through William W. Phelp's printing press in Independence, Missouri. It contained revelations, information, and news regarding the Church.

444. Missouri mobs burned William W. Phelps' printing press and Algernon Sidney Gilbert's storehouse in the summer of 1834 because they did not want the Saints to have a storehouse or be able to publish their beliefs and revelations. On July 23, 1834, the citizens of Missouri held a meeting regarding the members of the Church. At the meeting, they concluded that they needed to drive the Mormons from Jackson County. The leaders of the meeting went to Bishop Edward Partridge, William W. Phelps, Algernon Sidney Gilbert, and several other LDS Church leaders in Missouri and demanded that they leave Jackson County, stop printing "The Evening and Morning Star," close their storehouse, and agree that no Mormons ever return to Jackson County. These men refused.

445. After the mob actions, "The Evening and Morning Star" was not published again.

446. After the mobs' actions, the mobs returned to the Missouri Church leaders and forced them to sign an agreement to leave Jackson County on or before January 1, 1834. The agreement said that all Mormons

must be gone by April 1, 1834, or there would be more violence. If the Mormons would leave, the mobs agreed to keep the peace until then.

447. Regardless of promised peace, mobs in Missouri stole the Saints' land, property, and possessions. On the night of October 31, 1833, a mob of about forty to fifty armed men attacked a branch of the Church west of Big Blue. They unroofed and partially demolished ten Mormon homes. They whipped, beat, and even killed a few LDS men. Women and children fled to the wilderness for protection.

448. In August 1833, an article called "Mormonism" was published in the *Western Monitor*. It recounted the meeting of the citizens in Jackson County. Based on what was said in the meeting, the Saints were not hated because they had committed any crimes or done any wrong. They were hated for their religion and beliefs only. The Missouri citizens hated the Mormons purely based on their beliefs and their influences on Missouri slaves. Missouri was a slave state. Saints were kind to the slaves, and the citizens of Missouri did not like that.

449. On February 24, 1834, Joseph Smith received the revelation to organize a group of Saints to go to Missouri and regain the stolen possessions of the victims. Today, we refer to this journey as "Zion's Camp." The revelation can be found in Doctrine and Covenants 103:29–40.

450. Zion's Camp was the attempt to regain the land, arms, and possessions of the Missouri Saints. At the time, Zion's Camp was called the "Army of Israel" or the "Camp of Israel."

451. The governor of Missouri, Daniel Dunklin, arranged for the Saints to be guarded on their journey back to Jackson County. Daniel Dunklin ordered Colonel Lucas to make the mobs return the stolen weapons and arms to the Saints. He also spoke with the attorney general about prosecuting the mob for criminal actions, but the mob was very powerful. The attorney general advised them not to prosecute the mobs for fear of the consequences.

ZION'S CAMP WAS ORIGINALLY CALLED THE "ARMY OF ISRAEL."

452. According to a letter written by William W. Phelps, it was not just the Saints who were forced to leave Jackson County. Any citizen who refused to take up arms against the Mormons was also persecuted and forced to leave the county.

453. The army of Zion's Camp consisted of about 150 people. It was mostly men, although there were a few women and even some children! Zion's Camp was led by Joseph Smith.

454. Zion's Camp was a 900-mile journey from Kirtland to Jackson County mostly on foot. Some Saints came from other locations.

455. Members of Zion's Camp had morning and nightly prayers every day. Every person participated.

456. The weather during the journey was warm. It caused their feet to become blistered, bloody, and sore.

457. Spies repeatedly tried infiltrating Zion's Camp to harass the Saints and even steal the camp's horses.

458. At one point during the journey, the camp got stuck in thick mud that reached the top of their boots. They had to pull the wagons out of the mud using ropes. It was a challenging and strenuous task.

459. During the journey, the group began murmuring against Joseph. Then one day, their horses were all too weak to travel. Joseph told the group that the Lord was trying to teach them because of their complaints. They repented, the horses were healed, and the journey continued.

460. George A. Smith wrote that while it seemed like everybody else murmured against the Prophet during their trip, Joseph Smith never complained once. He was always positive and cheery, unless the brethren needed a rebuking.

461. There were so many mob threats against Zion's Camp that many feared for their lives. Joseph Smith prophesied in the name of the Lord that they would finish the journey unharmed by mobs. It was true! The Prophet later wrote about this, claiming that those who marched with Zion's Camp could physically see angels of God helping them and protecting them along their journey.

462. A mob led by Samuel C. Owens and James Campbell was plotting to kill all of Zion's Camp. James Campbell swore, "The eagles and turkey buzzards shall eat my flesh if I do not fix Joe Smith and his army so that their skins will not hold shucks before two days are passed." On their way, the mob took a ferry to cross the river. The boat sunk. Seven of the twelve men drowned. Owens barely survived, but James Campbell's body floated down the river a few miles and got stuck in a pile of drift wood, where (in Joseph's words): "the eagles and buzzards, ravens, crows and wild animals eat his flesh from his bones, to fulfil his own words,

and left him a horrible skeleton of God's vengeance" (Joseph Smith, in *History of the Church*, 1:525).

463. More mobs tried reaching Zion's Camp. One night, a mob came close to entering the camp. Suddenly, a huge hail and lightning storm caused a lot of damage to the mob. Their horses ran away or got sick, and their weapons were ruined. Luckily, though, no damage was sustained during this storm to Zion's Camp, the people in the camp, or their weapons.

464. While traveling through towns during the day, the army of Zion's Camp spread out so the civilians would not grow suspicious and start conflict.

465. Joseph Smith sometimes went by the name "Squire Cook" during the journey, to keep mobs from attacking Zion's Camp if they found out who he was.

466. One day, the people in the camp were hungry. Some of the brethren found what they thought were turtle eggs. They brought them back for the camp to eat. Joseph warned that they were actually snake eggs and told them not to eat them or they would get sick. Several ignored the Prophet and were severely ill the entire next day.

467. During their travels, Zion's Camp visited several ancient mounds from the former inhabitants of the country. One morning, Joseph and some of the men went up on a high mound near the river. On top were three altars, one on top of the other, according to ancient religious tradition. There were also signs of human remains. The men dug a hole and found the almost-complete skeleton of a man with the stone point of an arrow in his chest.

468. Joseph Smith then had a vision and saw that the man whose skeleton they found was a white Lamanite. He was a large, thick-set man. Joseph said he was a righteous man who obeyed God. His name was Zelph. He was a chief warrior under the Prophet Onandagus. During Zelph's lifetime, the Lamanites were not living righteously, but Zelph was still a righteous man. Instead, he lived among the Nephites. Zelph was killed in battle, fighting with the Nephites against the Lamanites.

469. In June 1834, James Foster became ill during the journey of Zion's Camp. He asked Joseph if he could stay behind, claiming he would die if he had to continue the expedition with his current health. Joseph prophesied that if Foster could be faithful and ride on a bed in the wagon, he would get better every day until he recovered. James Foster listened and he slowly regained his health every day.

470. Later that month, a mob was plotting to attack Zion's Camp. Just before the attack, one of the mob men was struck by lightning and killed. Another mobber accidentally cut off his hand in a freak accident while walking his horse. The mob retreated in fear that God was fighting for the Mormons, and they did not want to mess with Him.

471. One night, the guards of Zion's Camp saw lights across the river that looked like fires of approaching mobs. They panicked and woke Joseph, who investigated the lights. It was just the reflection of the moon on the trees. Joseph thought the guards' mistake was hilarious. He called the brethren to come see as well. They all laughed and were amused and relieved to know they were still safe.

472. Throughout the journey, Joseph frequently taught against harming or killing animals. He said God only allowed it when it is necessary for food. Joseph declared it God's will for peace between animals and humans. When they pitched their tents one day, they found three snakes. The men wanted to kill the snakes but Joseph forbade them. The brethren carried the snakes safely away from the camp on sticks.

JOSEPH OFTEN TAUGHT AGAINST HARMING OR NEEDLESSLY KILLING ANIMALS.

473. After several speeches to the brethren about protecting animals and leaving them unharmed, Joseph saw some of the brethren watching a squirrel in a tree. Joseph shot and killed the squirrel, and then he walked away. It may sound crazy, but the Prophet was testing the brethren. Orson Hyde picked up the squirrel and said they would cook it for food so it was not wasted. Joseph Smith was thrilled to know the brethren had listened to his teachings.

474. The squirrel was actually given to James Foster—the man who fell ill earlier in the trip and needed to lay in bed in a wagon—to eat.

475. By the end of June 1834, Zion's Camp had crossed most of Missouri. Rumor was spreading throughout the state. Many thought the Saints were coming to get violent revenge on the mobs.

476. Joseph and the brethren tried negotiating peacefully with the governor and political leaders of Missouri regarding getting the stolen property returned. These negotiations were ineffective and unsuccessful. The Missouri governor withdrew his promise to help the Saints with

obtaining their possessions. Joseph Smith decided it was best to disband Zion's Camp to avoid violence.

477.   Joseph Smith was fiercely criticized for his decision to dismiss Zion's Camp. Many of the army of Zion's Camp got sick with cholera shortly after. Unfortunately, fourteen members of Zion's Camp passed away from their illness.

478.   Joseph and Hyrum also got sick with cholera while attempting to heal those who were ill in the camp. They were in serious pain. They went to an area near camp and prayed repeatedly together that they would be healed. After a very long time, Hyrum told Joseph that he received revelation that they would be healed because of their mother's prayers for them. What Joseph and Hyrum did not realize was, at that exact moment, Lucy Mack Smith had a vision of her sons suffering with cholera and had been begging God to heal them. After Hyrum told Joseph about their mother, they were immediately healed. Joseph later told his mother that he and Hyrum had been spared so many times because Lucy was praying for their sake.

479.   Zion's Camp was disbanded on July 25, 1834, during the cholera outbreak.

480.   Joseph Smith returned to Kirtland after Zion's Camp with intense persecution from the Saints there. However, those who participated in Zion's Camp had increased faith in the Prophet. In fact, many of the original Quorum of the Twelve and the Quorum of the Seventy were picked from those who marched with Zion's Camp.

KIRTLAND TEMPLE DEDICATION

481.   On January 21, 1836, Joseph Smith saw a vision where God revealed the administration of ordinances in preparation for the dedication of the Kirtland Temple. In this vision, Joseph saw his deceased older brother, Alvin, in the celestial kingdom. It was revealed to him that all who die without a knowledge of the gospel, who would have received it, will be heirs of the celestial kingdom of God.

482.   It was also revealed through this vision that all children who die before the age of accountability—eight years old—are saved in the celestial

kingdom. This vision and revelation can be found in Doctrine and Covenants 137.

483. The Kirtland Temple construction was completed in 1836.

484. The early Saints described the Kirtland Temple exterior walls as a blue color. The wall color has since faded. The doors were olive green. It was apparently a very colorful temple.

485. The third floor of the Kirtland Temple included Joseph Smith's office, along with five school rooms. The school rooms comprised what was called the "Kirtland High School." Students of the Kirtland High School ranged from six years old to thirty years old. The youngest students were taught subjects such as basic reading, writing, and math. The oldest students could learn foreign or ancient languages.

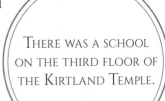

THERE WAS A SCHOOL ON THE THIRD FLOOR OF THE KIRTLAND TEMPLE.

486. While some of the saving temple ordinances were partially introduced in the Kirtland Temple, they were not all fully restored and completed until Nauvoo. The Kirtland Temple was less of an LDS temple by modern definition; it was more of a meetinghouse or chapel.

487. The Kirtland Temple was dedicated on Sunday, March 27, 1836, by the Prophet Joseph Smith.

488. On the day of the temple dedication, about 500–600 people lined up outside before the doors even opened to the public. There was so much curiosity and excitement.

489. About 1,000 people attended the Kirtland Temple dedication. Not everyone fit in the first-floor room, so some had to go upstairs while others were not able to attend at all.

490. The attendees sang "The Spirit of God," which was written by William W. Phelps.

491. The Saints in attendance of the Kirtland Temple dedication beheld visions and spoke in tongues. Many saw the face of Jesus Christ; others saw angels inside and outside the temple.

492. Joseph Smith saw a vision of the Quorum of the Twelve Apostles and many others who were present sitting on thrones in the celestial kingdom. Joseph also saw Jesus Christ's Apostles in the celestial kingdom. He saw visions of William McLellin and Brigham Young teaching the gospel

in foreign lands. He saw a vision of the armies of heaven protecting the Saints on their journey to Zion.

493.   The dedication of the temple was so incredible that those in attendance did not leave the temple until two in the morning!

494.   Joseph once wrote that after the Kirtland Temple dedication and solemn assembly, the Church had a season of overwhelming peace and joy.

495.   Soon after the dedication of the Kirtland Temple, Joseph Smith held a meeting where he warned the brethren to beware of evil people who sat in that very congregation. If those people did not repent, they would apostatize and eventually desire to kill the Prophet. Shortly after, his prophecy was fulfilled and many of the brethren dissented and became enemies of the Church.

496.   Joseph had a vision of this prophecy. It was so painful for Joseph to watch his friends betray him that he begged God to take it from him. He did get a break from the vision, but it returned.

497.   On April 3, 1836, Joseph Smith and Oliver Cowdery prayed privately at the pulpit asking the Lord to accept the Kirtland Temple as His house. Jesus Christ appeared to them and accepted the Kirtland House of the Lord.

498.   Christ stood on pure gold on the breastwork of the pulpit. Joseph and Oliver described Him as having white hair, with a voice like roaring water, and a countenance brighter than the sun.

499.   After the vision of Jesus Christ closed, another vision opened. Moses appeared to Joseph Smith and Oliver Cowdery and bestowed upon them the keys of the gathering of Israel from the four quarters of the earth and leading the last tribes from land of the north.

500.   After the vision of Moses closed, Elias appeared in a vision to Joseph Smith and Oliver Cowdery. He committed them the keys of the dispensation of the gospel of Abraham. Elias said the early Saints and all generations of Saints after them would be blessed.

501.   Finally, Elijah, who was taken from Earth without tasting death, appeared to Joseph and Oliver. He said the time had come for Malachi's prophecy that Elijah would come again to turn the hearts of the fathers to their children, and the children to their fathers to be fulfilled. He bestowed upon Joseph Smith and Oliver Cowdery the keys to this dispensation of the fulness of times. The keys bestowed upon them contained the priesthood authority to perform ceremonies that bind

on earth and in heaven, such as baptisms for the dead, endowments, and sealings.

502. When the Saints left Kirtland, one of the apostates of the Church disrespectfully used the Kirtland Temple building as a barn. It held cattle and livestock. He also filled the sacred pulpits with hay and straw.

ONE OF THE APOSTATES OF THE CHURCH LATER USED THE KIRTLAND TEMPLE AS A BARN.

JOSEPH'S EGYPTIAN MUMMIES

503. A man named Michael H. Chandler came to Kirtland to exhibit four Egyptian human mummies. He also had two rolls of papyrus with ancient Egyptian writing. He wished to find somebody who could translate the papyrus writing, and those around town told him to go to Joseph Smith. Joseph did correctly translate a few characters, and Michael Chandler gave him a certificate stating he correctly translated them.

504. Chandler tried selling Joseph the mummies and papyrus. Joseph really wanted the papyrus, not so much the mummies. He could purchase one only if he purchased both. Some Saints bought the mummies and papyrus for the Church, and Joseph spent months translating the papyrus.

505. Michael H. Chandler claimed that three of the mummies were that of Abraham, Abimelech (King of the Philistines), and Joseph of Egypt. It caused a great deal of excitement surrounding the mummies in Kirtland. Joseph debunked these rumors, though, and he even gave descriptions of how these mummies actually died and were buried.

506. The writing on the papyrus, however, was written in part by Abraham and Joseph of Egypt.

507. The mobs in Ohio threatened to steal the mummies several times but never did.

508. When Joseph Smith died, Lucy Mack Smith inherited the Egyptian artifacts. She displayed them to visitors in Nauvoo to provide for herself until her death. When she died, Joseph Smith III and Emma's second husband sold the artifacts.

509. Many believe Joseph received these translations and published them in the Pearl of Great Price as the Book of Abraham. It was recently discovered by modern scholars who studied the original papyrus scrolls that there are no similarities between the Book of Abraham and the original papyrus scrolls. Henry B. Eyring once suggested that one of the reasons Joseph received those scrolls was to open his mind to the idea of seeking the revelations now found in the Pearl of Great Price.

CRISIS IN KIRTLAND

510. The Church formed a bank called the Kirtland Safety Society Bank. Joseph Smith was the cashier of the bank. He handled day-to-day affairs but had no control over big decisions made regarding the bank.

511. Several members of the Church lost faith in Joseph Smith because they did not like Joseph telling them how to handle their finances. They left the Church, and some began spreading rumors about Joseph Smith.

512. All the drama led to Joseph's resignation from the bank. The Bank Directors hired Warren Parrish to replace Joseph. Warren Parrish was Joseph Smith's scribe. After working at the bank for a while, Warren Parrish accused Joseph of counterfeiting bank notes in exchange for money. Then Joseph accused Parrish of the same. These accusations led to dissention and division among Church members and apostates. Historians have recently discovered stock ledgers from the Kirtland Safety Society Bank records that demonstrate that Warren Parrish was responsible for the counterfeited bank notes.

513. Warren Parrish stood up during a meeting at the Kirtland Temple and publicly denounced the Prophet in front of him and dozens of Saints. Parrish cursed the Prophet that he would soon die. Disbelief, confusion, and chaos erupted in the temple. Joseph and the other Church leaders were devastated.

514. In this moment of alarm, Joseph calmly went to Heber C. Kimball in the room and whispered in his ear that it was time for Kimball to go on a mission to England for the salvation of the Church. Heber C. Kimball left on a mission to England soon after.

515. Joseph became extremely ill. Many of the Saints worried Parrish's curse of the Prophet's death would become a reality. Luckily, Joseph Smith recovered.

516. In 1837 in the United States, there was a lot of rumor and speculation about the banks around the country. It caused financial panic and crisis all over the country. Numerous banks had to be closed. Kirtland, Ohio, was no exception. The Kirtland Society Bank was soon shut down as well.

517. About one-third of Church leadership left the Church during the Kirtland Bank Crisis of 1837.

518. In November 1837, the Church's printing press in Kirtland was burned down by the mobs.

519. In January 1838, the mob actions and persecution in Kirtland became so harsh that Joseph Smith and Sidney Rigdon both decided to move themselves and their families to Far West, Missouri.

520. Just before Joseph Smith left Kirtland, he held a meeting with the brethren. At the end of the meeting, he told them he would certainly see them again because God promised that Joseph would live at least five more years. He said this in 1838; he was murdered six years later in 1844.

521. That night, Joseph was warned by the Spirit to move himself and his family to Missouri immediately. They barely had time to grab their beds and enough clothing before they left in the middle of the night.

522. The mobs followed Joseph Smith and Sidney Rigdon out of town and tried to shoot them multiple times. The Smiths and Rigdons stayed in the same public house with the mobs on two different occasions. The mob examined the families while they thought Joseph was asleep, and they did not recognize him or Rigdon. They left them unharmed. The mobs knew Joseph and Sidney were in Kirtland. It is a miracle they did not recognize them when seeking to kill them!

> AFTER A WARNING FROM THE SPIRIT, JOSEPH AND HIS FAMILY FLED KIRTLAND IN THE MIDDLE OF THE NIGHT.

523. Joseph Smith and his family arrived in Far West, Missouri, in March 1838.

524. Brigham Young and his family also fled for their lives from Kirtland to Missouri in 1838.

525. Oliver Cowdery associated with some of those who questioned Joseph Smith and the Church leadership after the Kirtland Bank Crisis and financial issues, but Oliver and most of the dissenters never questioned the doctrine and truthfulness of the gospel, only the character of Joseph Smith. Charges of dishonesty and attempting to defame the character of Joseph Smith were brought against Oliver Cowdery at disciplinary court on April 12, 1838. Oliver Cowdery refused to attend and was therefore excommunicated.

526. Even though Oliver Cowdery attended the Methodist Church in the years following his excommunication, he never denied the truthfulness of The Church of Jesus Christ of Latter-day Saints or his visions of angels and with Joseph Smith. After the Prophet's death, many were surprised to hear how highly Oliver Cowdery spoke of Joseph Smith and how sad he was to hear of his martyrdom. Oliver was re-baptized into The Church of Jesus Christ of Latter-day Saints in 1848 by Orson Hyde. Cowdery admits in one of his letters to the Church that he was too prideful to come back at first, but he always knew the Church was true. Oliver wrote that he desired no high position in the Church or a big ceremony, only to be re-baptized. He died two years after his re-baptism.

527. The entire Whitmer family, including Whitmer in-laws (like Oliver Cowdery), either left or were excommunicated from the Church during the Kirtland Bank Crisis. They believed Joseph was a fallen prophet, that he restored the true Church but had fallen away and become evil. Most of the eleven witness of the Book of Mormon were part of the Whitmer family. They never denied seeing the plates and that the Book of Mormon was true. Even when some anti-Mormons would try tricking them into saying it was false, all the witnesses of the Book of Mormon held true to their word about the truthfulness of the Book of Mormon.

MISSOURI

528. On July 20, 1831, the Lord revealed to Joseph Smith the exact location of Zion (the New Jerusalem) in Jackson County, Missouri. Zion is going to be the gathering spot of the Latter-day Saints when Jesus Christ comes again.

529. About five miles south of Jameson, Missouri, is a place Joseph Smith named "Adam-ondi-Ahman." He called it Adam-ondi-Ahman because it is where Adam and Eve lived after they were cast out of the Garden of Eden.

530. Wrestling was a common activity among the LDS men in Missouri. They would organize a ring with two competitors. They would try throwing the other out of the ring before they were thrown out. Joseph was a strong and talented wrestler. He reportedly defeated the best wrestler in Daviess County, Missouri, three times.

> JOSEPH REPORTEDLY DEFEATED THE BEST WRESTLER IN DAVIESS COUNTY, MISSOURI, THREE TIMES.

531. Howard Coray was a crippled, lightweight man who was good friends with Joseph Smith. Joseph told Howard he would love to wrestle him if Howard were larger. Howard told him to do it anyway. Joseph was a very large man and a strong wrestler. When the two men wrestled, Joseph accidentally broke Howard's leg. Joseph felt horrible for what happened. Howard compared himself to Jacob, who wrestled with an angel and then received a blessing. He asked Joseph for a blessing, which he received. Joseph blessed Howard that he would find a wife that would cling to him, be suitable to his crippled condition, and that together they would have many children. This blessing was fulfilled when Howard met his wife, Martha Jane.

532. Martha Jane Coray, with some assistance from Howard, later helped Lucy Mack Smith write her autobiography. Lucy Mack Smith's book was the first autobiography or biography written regarding the Prophet Joseph Smith. It is regarded as the most intimate as well, as it was written by the Prophet's mother.

533. In January 1831, the Saints were commanded to live the law of consecration. The law of consecration required Saints to give some of their belongings to the Church so they could help take care of other members of the Church. The purpose of the law of consecration was to remove the inequality between the rich and the poor, if lived perfectly. It was a slippery slope, though, because some gave what they were commanded, while some secretly kept some things for themselves.

534. On July 8, 1838, the Lord revealed that because of their pride, the Saints were not living the law of consecration correctly. He revoked the law of consecration commandment and instead revealed the law of tithing. The law of tithing requires the Saints to donate ten percent of their income to the Church, and the Church uses that money for things such as humanitarian aid, missionary work, and building temples and churches. The law of tithing is still lived by the Saints today.

THE LAW OF CONSECRATION WAS REPLACED BY THE LAW OF TITHING IN 1838.

535. Word got around to Missouri residents about the LDS belief that Jackson County was Zion. Rumors caused a lot of tension between the Mormons and the other citizens, especially since the Saints believed the land was going to be given to them by God as the gathering place of the Second Coming of Jesus Christ.

536. Joseph Smith designed Zion with twenty-four church buildings (churches, administrative buildings, temples, etc.) at the center of town, with farms, agriculture, and homes surrounding them. This caused more problems between the Saints and the Jackson County residents, because the residents feared the Mormons were trying to take over.

537. MYTH: African Americans were not permitted to be baptized into The Church of Jesus Christ of Latter-day Saints in Missouri because the Church leaders were racist. FACT: African American men and women were not allowed to join the Church in Missouri because it was against the state law of Missouri, which was a slave state at the time.

The Church had been commanded to obey the laws of the land. That is the only reason why blacks were not allowed to be baptized into the Church. However, once the Saints moved to the free state of Illinois, all were welcome to join.

THE MORMON WAR

538. The growing Mormon population in Missouri could have meant growing Mormon political power. The citizens of Missouri did not want the Mormons to have any political influence in their state.

539. William Peniston, who was a candidate for state legislature in 1838, told the residents in Daviess County that if the Mormons voted in the election, everyone else would lose their suffrage. He also warned the Saints not to vote in the upcoming election or there would be repercussions.

540. Some Mormons ignored his warning and went to vote in the election in Gallatin, Missouri, on August 6, 1838. Around 200 citizens gathered to prevent the Saints from voting. It resulted in a violent fight. Many non-Mormons threatened to retrieve their guns and ammunition to kill the Saints, so the Mormons had to return to their homes without voting. This is believed by most historians to be the first act of violence in Missouri of what came to be known as "the Mormon War."

541. The term "Mormon War" is often used by modern scholars to describe the violence and mini civil war between the Mormons and non-Mormons in Missouri.

542. Further lies and rumors spread about the election day brawl that caused even more issues between the Mormons and non-Mormons in Missouri. There were several claims that the Mormons killed a few citizens during the violent fight, and vice versa. Joseph Smith and a few others rode to Adam-ondi-Ahman to investigate the claims. They discovered that nobody was killed in either party during the riot. However, several people on both sides were wounded.

543. The mob in Daviess County sent letters to militias in surrounding areas asking for assistance against the "violent Mormons." They claimed Joseph Smith had killed seven innocent men during the riot in Daviess

County, which was not true. Nobody died in the fight, and Joseph Smith was not there anyway. They asked the militias to come help kill "Joe Smith" and the rest of the Mormons.

544. The militias believed the claims and became enraged. They marched to Lucy Mack Smith's home, where Joseph Smith was. Joseph was writing an important document in another room in the house. At first, Lucy did not realize they were actually intending to kill her and her son.

545. Eight men from the group came to her door. She let them inside and offered them water and a place to sit. They refused, stating, "We do not choose to sit down; we have come to kill Joe Smith and all the Mormons." Lucy replied calmly, "Ah, what has Joseph Smith done, that you should want to kill him?" They replied, "He has killed seven men in Daviess County, we have come to kill him and all his church." Lucy answered, "He has not been in Daviess County, consequently the report must be false. Furthermore, if you should see him, you would not want to kill him" (Lucy Mack Smith, *The History of Joseph Smith by His Mother*, 232).

> JOSEPH WAS FALSELY ACCUSED OF KILLING SEVEN INNOCENT MEN IN DAVIESS COUNTY.

546. The men asserted that they knew the report had to be correct because it was sent directly to them, and they still planned to kill the Prophet and all his followers. Lucy asked if they intended to kill her too, they answered in the affirmative. She replied, again calmly, "Very well, I want you to act the gentleman about it, and do the job quick. Just shoot me down at once, then I shall be at rest; but I shall not like to be murdered by the inches." Her response shocked the officers, one of them said: "There it is again, you tell a Mormon that you will kill them, and they will always tell you 'that is nothing; kill us, we shall be happy'" (Lucy Mack Smith, *The History of Joseph Smith by His Mother*, 232).

547. At this very moment, Joseph walked into the room. Lucy introduced her son to the officers as "Joseph Smith, the Prophet." The men stared at Joseph Smith for a long time. Joseph smiled and shook each of their hands. Lucy was right when she said that if the officers would meet him, they would not want to kill him. When Joseph shook their hands and spoke with them about the Church's beliefs, views, persecutions, and so on, they knew he was an honest and innocent man. Joseph also nobly

reminded them that any person guilty of breaking the law should be tried and convicted by the law before they are killed.

548. After this discussion with the officers, Joseph mentioned it was time for him to get home and take care of Emma. Two of the men sprung up and insisted on escorting him home to protect him. They and a few more officers helped the Prophet get home safely.

549. Three of the militiamen remained in Lucy's home a few minutes after the Prophet and the other officers left. Lucy overheard a conversation between them before they departed. First Officer: "Did you not feel strangely when Smith took you by the hand? I never felt so in my life." Second Officer: "I could not move. I would not harm a hair on that man's head for the whole world." Third Officer: "This is the last time you will catch me coming to kill Joe Smith, or the Mormons either." First Officer: "I guess this is about my last expedition against this place. I never saw a more harmless, innocent appearing man than the 'Mormon Prophet.'" Second Officer: "That story about his killing them men is all a d—d lie; there is no doubt of it; and we have had this trouble for nothing; but they will never fool me in this way again, I'll warrant them." The officers then disbanded the militia. However, tension in Missouri still remained (Lucy Mack Smith, *The History of Joseph Smith by His Mother*, 233).

550. Another claim was that Judge Adam Black was forming a mob against the Mormons. Joseph Smith, along with about one hundred armed men, came to the judge's house and had him sign a document disavowing any connection to the mobs. Adam Black refused. Eventually, though, he wrote and signed his own document stating he was not involved in any mobs and would keep the peace with the Mormons as long as the Mormons were peaceful. Judge Adam Black later stated that he only did so because he felt threatened by Joseph and the other armed men.

551. Joseph and the others went to several other rumored leaders of the mobs and had them sign similar documents disavowing mobs and violence against the Saints.

552. There was a meeting held at Lyman Wight's home between Church leaders and Missouri political leaders. Every person agreed to report all lawbreakers to the authorities and keep the peace between the Mormons and non-Mormons. Joseph Smith and the other Church leaders returned to their homes in Missouri, expecting peace.

553. Henry Root was a non-Mormon and the major land-owner in Caldwell County. He visited Far West in the spring of 1838 and sold most of his lots in De Witt, Missouri, to a few Mormons who gathered there to colonize it. Missourians were afraid of the growing Mormon population and placed the question of whether Mormons should be allowed to colonize in De Witt on the August 6, 1838 Election Ballot.

554. The majority voted to expel the Mormons from De Witt, especially since the Mormons themselves were violently prohibited from voting. A committee was sent to De Witt to drive the Saints out of town. The Mormon colonizers refused, claiming they had rights as American citizens to settle wherever they wanted in the country.

555. As tensions rose in other counties between Mormons and non-Mormons, almost all non-Mormons in Missouri desired to remove the Saints from De Witt. It led to further mob violence on Mormon families. Many Mormons were even killed.

556. The Church leaders in De Witt sent a letter to Governor Lilburn Boggs for assistance. Boggs refused to get involved. Finally, on October 11, Church leaders decided to leave De Witt. They traveled to Far West, where the Prophet lived at the time.

557. On their way from De Witt to Far West, some Saints starved to death. Since the mob was following close behind, there was no time to build coffins or hold proper funerals for the deceased. They had to bury them in unmarked graves on the side of the road and keep going. Some lost parents, spouses, children, or siblings and then had to bury them by the wayside without a casket or funeral in order to save their own lives and the rest of their family.

558. Once in Far West, the De Witt Saints had no houses to stay in. Many had to stay in tents. Those who did not have tents had to sleep outside with blankets only, and some did not even have the warmth and pleasure of blankets . . . just the cold ground.

559. According to Hyrum Smith, some Mormon men were taken from their families and whipped and beaten so badly that they had to wear makeshift adult diapers because their severe injuries caused temporary bowel incontinence.

560. Any acts of Mormon self-defense against the mobs only further enraged the mobs and led to more violence.

561. On October 25, 1838, Captain Nehemiah Comstock came into a few areas in Missouri (including Haun's Mill) and demanded the Mormons surrender all their guns.

562. The militias who were supposed to protect the Saints often had troops that desired instead to join the mobs because they hated the Mormons too, according to General Alexander Doniphan, who led one of the militias. Luckily, most of their superiors ordered them to protect the Saints. They did so, at least while on duty.

563. The mobs tried coercing the Saints into committing crimes so they would go to jail. They were unsuccessful. Instead, many of the mob members burned their own homes and fields. Then they went to the authorities and claimed the Mormons were the arsonists behind their lost property.

564. The mobs in Missouri stole Mormon cattle and hogs. Threatening their lives, the mobs took Latter-day Saint men, women, and children as prisoners. They whipped them, gashed their skin with tree branches, and tied them to trees. The prisoners were forced to eat the tree bark to keep from starving to death.

565. The mobs robbed Mormon houses as they took the residents hostage, threatening their lives if they did not comply and vow to leave Missouri.

566. Joseph Smith was a huge mob target in Missouri. Some men in Daviess County, Missouri, offered a cash reward of $1,000 to the man who would bring them Joseph Smith's scalp. The Prophet was once watering his horse at Shoal Creek and jumped at the sound of mob gunshots toward him, which he had to flee from quickly to save his life.

> SOME MEN OFFERED A CASH REWARD OF $1,000 TO THE MAN WHO WOULD BRING THEM JOSEPH SMITH'S SCALP.

567. A militia commanded by Samuel Bogart was ordered to patrol an unincorporated territory nicknamed "Bunkham's Strip." They did not obey orders, however. Samuel Bogart and his militia passed the Bunkham's Strip into southern Caldwell County where they harassed the Mormons. The Saints were unable to defend themselves because they were forced to give up their arms.

568. Word reached Far West about the mob in Caldwell County, and a group of armed Mormon men assembled together to defend the Saint

prisoners. Upon arrival of the militia's camp on Crooked River, a battle broke out between them. Only one in the Missouri militia was killed in the combat, and his name was Moses Rowland. Two Mormon men were killed, Gideon Carter and David W. Patten (one of the Quorum of the Twelve). There were nine Mormons wounded (including Patten at first, but he later died from his wounds). This encounter is now referred to as the Battle of Crooked River.

569. The lies and rumors about the Mormon involvement at the Battle of Crooked River reached Missouri Governor Lilburn W. Boggs. He believed the Mormons to be evil, violent murderers. He then issued what came to be known as the "Extermination Order."

570. On October 27, 1838, Missouri Governor Lilburn Boggs issued the Missouri Executive Order 44, also known as "the Extermination Order." The most infamous part of the order read as follows: "The Mormons must be treated as enemies, and must be exterminated or driven from the state if necessary for the public peace" (Missouri Executive Order 44, Lilburn Boggs).

571. Lilburn W. Boggs did not run for re-election. Many of the Missourians, Mormon and non-Mormon, believed Boggs's Extermination Order to be unfair and unwarranted. Boggs likely knew that he would not get re-elected.

HAUN'S MILL MASSACRE

572. Haun's Mill was a small town in Missouri. The population was mostly—if not all—members of the Church.

573. Multiple mobs gathered around Haun's Mill to attack. About twenty-eight Mormon men armed themselves in self-defense. At first, the Mormons were able to negotiate a peace treaty between them and the mobs. There was peace for about two days.

574. The Haun's Mill Massacre is likely the most infamous act of mob violence on the Latter-day Saints in Missouri.

575. The massacre occurred only three days following Governor Boggs's Extermination Order.

576. On October 30, 1838, at approximately 4:00 p.m., a militia of about 240 marched into Haun's Mill. David Evans, one of the Church leaders in Haun's Mill, tried negotiating peace with the militia, but he was unsuccessful.

577. The militia ignored the cries for peace as they marched into Haun's Mill. Many women and children ran into the woods when they saw the militia coming. Most of the men ran into the blacksmith's shop.

578. The militia leader, Nehemiah Comstock, fired a gun in the air. The gunshot was followed by a few seconds of eerie silence. Then all at once, the militia fired about one hundred rifles into the blacksmith's shop, which was not a good shelter. The blacksmith's shop had gaps between some of the logs of the building. It was easy for the militia to shoot right through the gaps. The massacre had begun.

579. The militia robbed their houses. They stole clothing, tents, and other possessions from the Mormons' homes.

580. The militiamen assaulted several Mormon women.

581. One Latter-day Saint man was forced to give up his own gun, and then he was shot with it. Then, one of the militiamen cut up the man's body from head to toe with a corn cutter.

582. Some of the militiamen followed the Saints who fled to the woods and shot and killed some of them as well.

SEVENTEEN SAINTS WERE KILLED AT HAUN'S MILL, THEIR AGES RANGING FROM SEVEN TO SIXTY-TWO.

583. Some people barely survived the attack by pretending to be dead after being shot or injured.

584. The ambush lasted around thirty minutes to an hour.

585. As a result of the attack on Haun's Mill, seventeen Latter-day Saints were killed. The victims ranged from ages seven to sixty-two.

586. The survivors of the Haun's Mill Massacre had to bury their loved ones quickly, with no funeral and no coffins, because they feared for their lives. They needed to flee without a chance to get proper closure from this traumatic event.

587. MYTH: Since the Haun's Mill Massacre occurred only a few days following Governor Boggs's Extermination Order, it is easy to assume the militia that attacked Haun's Mill was only following the governor's

order. FACT: This is a common misconception. Back then, news traveled a lot slower than it does today. The governor's order did not reach the Caldwell County militia who attacked Haun's Mill until after the massacre occurred.

588. The victims at Haun's Mill had absolutely no involvement with the Mormon War or the Battle of Crooked River. They were innocent victims of merciless assault and slaughter.

589. Many people criticized Joseph Smith after the Haun's Mill Massacre. They argued that if he were really a prophet of God, he would have warned the residents of Haun's Mill to leave before it happened. According to Lucy Mack Smith, though, three weeks before the tragedy, Joseph told a messenger to urge the brethren at Haun's Mill to move their families into the city of Far West as soon as possible. The messenger was Jacob Haun, who owned the mill. He never relayed the Prophet's warning to the brethren in Haun's Mill, likely because he did not want to lose the residents and workers of his mill and found Joseph's request unreasonable. Lucy wrote that if they had been properly warned, it would have saved their lives.

590. Despite Jacob Haun's refusal to advise the Saints at Haun's Mill to leave, some Saints received their own warning from God. One resident of Haun's Mill named John Reed had a dream three nights prior to the attack. He dreamt of the nearby creek running red with blood. He knew this was a warning from the Spirit, and he immediately moved himself and his family out of Haun's Mill, which saved his life and the lives of his wife and children.

591. General Lucas forced all the Saints in Far West to give up their arms and sign away their land to pay for the Mormon War. The Saints all had to camp outside Far West because they were kicked out of their homes.

JOSEPH AND OTHERS TAKEN AS PRISONERS OF WAR

592. Colonel George Hinkle was a member of the Church and commander of the Mormon forces. His superior was General Samuel Lucas, who

ordered Hinkle to give up Joseph Smith and other Church leaders to be tried and punished, along with other demands.

593. On October 31, 1838, Colonel Hinkle came to the Mormon camp and requested Joseph Smith, Parley P. Pratt, Sidney Rigdon, Lyman Wight, and George W. Robinson to come meet with General Samuel Lucas and negotiate peace. He assured the men that General Lucas had pledged not to abuse them and that they would be protected. They agreed.

594. When they arrived, they discovered that General Lucas and several armed militiamen were there. Joseph Smith requested they talk about restoring peace. Colonel Hinkle then said, "These are the prisoners I agreed to deliver up." General Lucas brandished his sword and said, "Gentlemen, you are my prisoners. There is no time for talking at the present. You will march into camp" (Joseph Smith, in *History of the Church*, 4:1635). Chaos erupted among the surrounding militiamen. They cheered, screamed, and laughed. About 500 men in the militia cocked their guns, and a few even shot at Joseph and the other Church leaders.

> JOSEPH SMITH AND OTHER CHURCH LEADERS WERE HELD AS PRISONERS OF WAR BY GENERAL SAMUEL LUCAS FOR ALMOST SIX MONTHS.

595. Colonel George Hinkle betrayed the Prophet Joseph Smith. From this point on, Joseph Smith and the others were held captive and wrongfully treated as traitors and prisoners of war for almost six months.

596. The following day, Colonel Hinkle came to Hyrum Smith's house with several more armed soldiers. He broke into the house and forced Hyrum to come with them as a prisoner as well. Hyrum initially refused because he and his family were sick. He needed to take care of them. Colonel Hinkle did not care and threatened Hyrum and his family's lives if he did not come immediately.

597. Lyman Wight, one of the fellow prisoners, later stated that the militia had no reasoning behind capturing Hyrum except that he was the brother of Joseph Smith.

598. When Joseph and Hyrum were captured, a messenger was sent to the Smith house to tell Joseph Smith Sr., Lucy Mack Smith, and their youngest daughter, Lucy, that if they wanted to see their sons/brothers ever again, they needed to go to them immediately. They were in wagons

set to leave in only a few minutes for Independence, Missouri, and would likely not come back alive. Joseph Smith Sr. was beside himself because he was too ill to go say goodbye to his sons. However, both women left promptly to catch the wagons before they departed with Joseph and Hyrum.

599. When the two women arrived, a large crowd was surrounding the wagons. The crowd was so dense, the women could not move any closer than about one hundred yards away from the wagon. Lucy Mack Smith shouted, asking if somebody could bring them to see her children one last time. One man offered to help pull them through the surrounding mob, who loudly threatened their lives as they passed through.

600. They reached the covered wagon where Hyrum was. The girls were only allowed to hold Hyrum's hand; they were not allowed to speak to each other or see each other. The man brought them to the wagon where Joseph was. Lucy Mack Smith held his hand and said, "Joseph, do speak to your poor mother once more. I cannot bear to go until I hear your voice." Joseph replied with a sob, "God bless you, mother" (Lucy Mack Smith, *The History of Joseph Smith by His Mother*, 258).

601. The mob was angry that the Prophet and his mother had spoken to each other against orders. The wagons sped off without warning, right as Joseph's little sister tried to give him a farewell kiss on his hand.

602. The Smith family was extremely agonized and worried for Joseph and Hyrum. They thought Joseph and Hyrum would undoubtedly be killed. Lucy prayed for her sons intensely and received this revelation, which comforted the entire Smith family: "Let your heart be comforted concerning your children, they shall not be harmed by their enemies; and in less than four years, Joseph shall speak before judges and great men of the land, for his voice shall be heard in their councils. And in five years from this time he will have power over all his enemies" (Lucy Mack Smith, *The History of Joseph Smith by His Mother*, 258). Within five years of this prophecy, Joseph Smith held a few powerful and influential positions Nauvoo, Illinois—Mayor of Nauvoo and Commander in Chief of the Nauvoo Legion (militia).

603. The day following the kidnapping of several Church leaders, General Lucas gave specific permission to his militiamen to attack the Mormons as they patrolled the streets of that area. According to Hyrum Smith, they abused the Mormons however they wanted that day. The militia

broke into Mormon homes, robbed them of their possessions and guns, raped the women, and destroyed many of the houses.

604. Once they had every prisoner in custody of the militia, General Lucas sentenced the prisoners to be shot in the public square of Far West, Missouri, the next morning by General Alexander Doniphan.

605. General Alexander Doniphan had been acquainted with Joseph Smith prior to this. He often used his military influence to help protect the Saints and also defended Joseph as his lawyer in several legal disputes. He never joined the Church but was very sympathetic toward the Mormons' mistreatment and helped defend them physically and legally on several occasions. He believed Joseph Smith and the other prisoners to be honest, good men.

606. At sunrise, the morning that Joseph and the other prisoners were sentenced to be shot, General Doniphan came to the prisoners. He shook each of their hands and told them he believed their sentence to be unjust and that he would not have any part of it. General Doniphan then went to General Lucas and said, "This is cold blooded murder . . . I will not obey your order. If you execute them, I will hold you responsible before an earthly tribunal so help me God!" (Joseph Smith, in *History of the Church*, 5:1829). General Doniphan ordered his brigade to leave. They all rode out of camp. It caused a huge uproar among the militiamen who remained. However, the lives of Joseph Smith and the other prisoners were saved that day.

607. General Lucas called a new court martial, and the prisoners were sentenced to be shot in Jackson County the next day instead. Wagons came to take the prisoners to a new location.

608. While the prisoners were getting into the wagons, an eager group of four or five men ran up with their guns aimed at the Prophet and the other Church leaders. They pulled the triggers, but miraculously, every single gun misfired. Since these men were not authorized to perform the execution, they were arrested for not obeying orders. The lives of Joseph, Hyrum, and the other Mormon prisoners were spared again.

A FEW MEN TRIED TO SHOOT THE CHURCH LEADERS, BUT EVERY ONE OF THEIR GUNS MISFIRED BEFORE THEY WERE ARRESTED FOR NOT OBEYING ORDERS.

609. The prisoners convinced General Lucas to allow them to visit their homes to get some extra clothes. Each prisoner was guarded by five or six men, and the prisoners were not allowed to speak to their families. They entered each house and ordered the wives to fetch clothes for their husbands within two minutes without speaking to them. Otherwise, the men would not get their clothes at all. Hyrum Smith wrote that his wife and children clung to his arms and legs in tears. It was heart-wrenching when he could not comfort them.

610. On their way to Richmond, Missouri, General Wilson told the prisoners they would be hung on the side of the road. General Clark, who was expected to receive the prisoners in Richmond, demanded that he do the killing himself. Thus, the prisoners were not hung on the side of the road, and their lives were spared once more.

611. While in the custody of General Clark, the prisoners were kept in an old log house. They were strongly guarded day and night. All seven prisoners were chained to each other by the ankles and wrists.

612. William Smith's brother-in-law and a few other friends came to visit the prisoners while they were in the custody of General Clark. They spoke with General Clark about how his prisoners were only religious leaders, not military men. Therefore, they could not be subject to a court martial execution like originally planned. Killing the prisoners this way would be illegal. General Clark spent the next week researching the military code of laws to see if he could get away with killing Joseph Smith and the others. He realized he could face legal consequences if he killed them.

613. He delivered the prisoners to the civil authorities instead, claiming they were guilty of crimes such as treason, murder, arson, and theft.

614. They held a trial for these accusations. Several witnesses lied on the witness stand and fabricated crimes committed against them by Joseph Smith and the other prisoners. The judge, Austin A. King, told the defendants to gather witnesses to help their case. Whenever any of the Mormon prisoners gave a list of witnesses for the court to subpoena, the militia would capture those witnesses and throw them in jail so they could not testify. A few other Mormons who could have been potential witnesses—like Brigham Young—fled to Illinois to avoid being thrown in jail.

615.   The militia captured sixty-seven Mormon men and threw them in jail so they could not testify in defense of the Prophet and the others.

616.   Those who were thrown in jail were told that if they would testify against Joseph Smith in the preliminary hearing of the trial, they would be released. Some of Joseph's closest friends, including William W. Phelps, reluctantly agreed to testify against the Prophet so they could go take care of their families and take them to Illinois for safety.

SIXTY-SEVEN MORMON MEN WERE IMPRISONED SO THAT THEY COULD NOT TESTIFY IN THE PROPHET'S DEFENCE.

617.   Joseph and the other prisoners with him at this time were kept in the courthouse of Judge Austin A. King. They were heavily guarded by about fifty men every night. The guards were usually the same men who had mobbed several Saints in Missouri. One night, the guards boasted vulgarly about robbing, violating, and murdering several Mormons in Far West. The prisoners had no choice but to listen to the filthy stories and words of the guards. None of the prisoners said anything at first, even though they were horrified and saddened. According to one of the prisoners, Parley P. Pratt, Joseph Smith stood up and spoke with a "voice of thunder, or as the roaring lion." The Prophet scolded the guards, "SILENCE, ye fiends of the infernal pit. In the name of Jesus Christ, I rebuke you and command you to be still; I will not live another minute and hear such language. Cease such talk, or you or I die THIS INSTANT!" (Parley P. Pratt, *The Autobiography of Parley Parker Pratt*, ch. 26).

618.   Joseph stood there majestically, calmly, without any weapons, with the "dignity of an angel," according to Pratt. The guards all lowered their weapons. Some even dropped to their knees and begged for Joseph's forgiveness. Parley Pratt wrote of this moment saying, "I have seen ministers of justice, clothed in magisterial robes, and criminals arraigned before them, while life was suspended on a breath . . . I have witnessed a Congress in solemn session to give laws to nations; I have tried to conceive kings, of royal courts, of thrones and crowns; and of emperors assembled to decide the fate of kingdoms; but dignity and majesty I have seen but once, as it stood in chains, at midnight, in a dungeon in an obscure village of Missouri" (Parley P. Pratt, *The Autobiography of Parley Parker Pratt*, ch. 26).

619. Joseph Smith once prophesied that one of the Elders would teach a sermon in Jackson County, Missouri, before the end of 1838. In late 1838, the Church leaders and saints were being thrown into prison or driven from the state of Missouri daily. The prophecy seemed highly unlikely to be fulfilled. On November 4, 1838, the prisoners were visited by a few curious non-Mormons. A woman came to the guards and asked which of the prisoners was the "Lord" whom the Mormons worshipped. The guards pointed to Joseph Smith. She went to Joseph and asked him if he professed to be the Lord and Savior. The Prophet responded that he only professed to be a man, and a minister set by Jesus Christ to preach the gospel. The woman was surprised, as she probably expected that he was a fraud who would try to claim the most possible recognition and glory by claiming to be God. She continued asking questions. Joseph preached to her and the others with her, and even some of the guards listened in. The group of visitors left with a testimony that Joseph Smith was a Prophet of God, and they audibly prayed for Joseph and the other prisoners' protection. Thus, the prophecy was fulfilled.

620. The defendants in the hearing did succeed in getting one witness for their case. His name was Charles Allen. As soon as he began speaking, a Methodist priest in the court grabbed Allen by the nape of his neck, pulled him from the witness stand, and shoved him out the door of the courthouse into a crowd of soldiers, and he screamed orders for them to shoot him. Luckily, Allen barely escaped with his life.

621. After the final (only!) Mormon witness of the hearing was thrown out, the court rose up and ordered the prisoners to be sent to jail for treason and murder. Those who were accused of treason or murder were not allowed bail, which is why the judge convicted them of such crimes. When the prisoners' defense lawyer asked why they would go to jail as innocent men, the judge responded, saying it was because they were Mormons. The judge said he planned to execute Governor Boggs's Extermination Order to the letter, whether they were innocent or not.

622. Joseph Smith, Hyrum Smith, Sidney Rigdon, Lyman Wight, Alexander McRae, and Caleb Baldwin were sent to Liberty Jail to await trial. Parley Pratt and the other remaining prisoners were sent to Richmond Jail to await trial.

LIBERTY JAIL

623. Joseph Smith was confined in Liberty Jail from December 1, 1838, until April 6, 1839, when they went to Gallatin, Missouri, for their trial. It was the coldest winter in the state of Missouri on record up to that point.

624. The entire building of Liberty Jail was fourteen feet by fourteen and a half feet, but the dungeon was shorter than six feet tall. Joseph and most of the other prisoners could not stand erect inside the dungeon.

625. While Joseph Smith was kept in Liberty Jail, Joseph Smith Sr. and William Smith felt they should move their families from Missouri to Illinois. Joseph Sr. was a little hesitant until he wrote to Joseph about it. The Prophet wrote back stating that the Lord revealed to Joseph Smith at Liberty that the Smiths and all the Saints needed to leave Missouri and go to Illinois for their safety.

> THE DUNGEON OF LIBERTY JAIL WAS SHORTER THAN SIX FEET TALL.

626. Joseph wrote several letters to the Church while he was in Liberty Jail. Some of them have become canonized as scripture and can be found in Doctrine and Covenants 121–123.

627. His incarceration at Liberty Jail, coupled with the Mormon War, can be argued to be the most trying time of Joseph's life. While in Liberty Jail, Joseph even questioned whether God had forsaken him and the Saints. It was then that he received the answer: "My son, peace be unto thy soul; thine adversity and thine afflictions shall be but a small moment; and then if thou endure it well, God shall exalt thee on high . . ." (Doctrine and Covenants 121:7–8). In this section, the Lord continues to give Joseph knowledge about why God allows us to suffer through certain

trials. He reveals that "all these things shall give thee experience, and shall be for thy good" (Doctrine and Covenants 122:7).

628. After this revelation, Joseph seemed to have a better understanding of this for the remainder of his life and forever dealt with trials differently. This revelation can be found in Doctrine and Covenants 121–123.

629. Emma visited Joseph in Liberty Jail several times, sometimes with their children. She visited multiple times in December 1838, before she had to flee to Illinois. Mary Fielding Smith, Hyrum's wife, visited Liberty Jail a few times too. Their son, Joseph Fielding Smith, was born while Hyrum was in captivity. The first time Hyrum met his son was when Mary brought him to Liberty Jail.

630. Joseph Fielding Smith received a baby blessing from his father, Hyrum, in Liberty Jail. Joseph Fielding Smith would grow up to become the sixth President of The Church of Jesus Christ of Latter-day Saints. His son, also named Joseph Fielding Smith (Jr.), became the tenth President of The Church of Jesus Christ of Latter-day Saints.

631. While in Liberty Jail, Joseph obtained some law books. He began studying a little bit of law there.

632. MYTH: Joseph and the others in Liberty Jail were never allowed to leave the underground dungeon. FACT: The prisoners were sometimes allowed to eat meals with the jail keepers upstairs, visit their attorneys, and go on guarded walks a few times as well. Notwithstanding, Liberty Jail was *not* by any means a pleasant place where the Mormon prisoners were treated fairly.

633. The dungeon was so dark that the prisoners often complained of sore eyes when their eyes were exposed to light.

634. The prisoners slept on straw. The food they were served was coarse and expired. It was usually leftover table scraps from the jail keepers. There was no chimney or way to build a fire in the dungeon. If they did build a fire, the dungeon would fill with smoke.

635. They had no means of obtaining warmth during the coldest winter in the state of Missouri on record at the time. Joseph wrote to Emma asking her to send blankets. She wrote back telling him that William McLellin (former member of the Quorum of the Twelve Apostles and friend of Joseph's, now excommunicated apostate) broke into Emma's home while the Prophet was away and stole all their blankets.

636. Poison was given to the prisoners on several occasions in their food. It was purposefully administered in small enough doses that the poison would not kill them, but large enough doses that it made them severely ill for days.

637. The guards conjured a plan: they refused to feed the prisoners anything except a little bit of bread for five days straight. Then, the only thing they gave them to eat on the sixth day was human flesh. It was the amputated arm of an African American, likely a Missouri slave. The jail keepers called it "Mormon beef." The guards were trying to coerce the prisoners to eat the flesh so they could sell the story to the newspapers, proving the Mormons to be evil monsters. The prisoners refused. Lyman Wight was the only prisoner to try even a little bit of it, and he got sick. The guards' plan was unsuccessful, so they did not tell anybody about the "Mormon beef."

638. When they did get visitors, the prisoners were not allowed to speak to them without a guard present. This was to prevent any escape attempts.

639. The prisoners tried escaping from the jail twice; both attempts were unsuccessful. They tried rushing the guards once, but they were caught and put back in the dungeon. The other time, they tried digging a hole in the ground, under the wall, and out the other side. They were caught again, and they were punished.

JOSEPH AND THE OTHER PRISONERS ONCE TRIED TO DIG A HOLE UNDER THE WALL TO ESCAPE.

640. Missourians came to Liberty Jail to observe the incarcerated Church leaders like zoo animals. They would insult and taunt them.

641. The prisoners were forced to use only small buckets that were kept in the dungeon for their latrine (nineteenth-century cheap toilet).

642. Judge Turnham believed the incarcerated Church leaders to be innocent. Since Sidney Rigdon was extremely sick toward the end of his time in jail, Judge Turnham was able to get him released on bail before anyone else was released.

643. Joseph wrote his last letter from Liberty Jail to Emma on April 4, 1839.

644. On April 6, 1839, the prisoners were taken to Gallatin for a hearing. Their grand jury consisted of drunken men.

645. At the hearing, Joseph and the others were indicted with treason and sent to trial in Columbia, Boone County, Missouri.

646. On the night of April 11, 1939, in custody of one of the judges, Joseph had a vision about one of his visiting friends, Stephen Markham. He awoke Markham and told him he needed to leave immediately on his horse or he would be killed by the mob if he waited too long to depart. Stephen Markham obeyed the Prophet's warning. The mob chased Markham for a while and shot at him, but he returned to Far West unharmed.

647. On their way to Boone County, the prisoners escaped to Illinois. Their guard was in a deep drunken sleep one night, and the prisoners ran away.

648. Joseph Smith receives some backlash for this today because many believe that as a prophet of God, he should have obeyed orders. Historians have recently discovered a receipt showing that Joseph and Hyrum bought a horse from one of the guards. It suggests that while they did escape in the middle of the night, they were permitted to leave (at least by one guard).

649. The horse that Joseph and Hyrum bought was named Medley. They alternated riding the horse and walking the horse until they reached Quincy.

650. Joseph Smith and the other prisoners at Liberty Jail had escaped or were released by April 16, 1839.

651. The prisoners had to walk 170 miles to get to Quincy while they were weak, tired, and hungry.

652. On his way to Quincy, Joseph was spotted by a man named Dimick Huntington. He described the Prophet as having boots with holes in them, ripped pants, and a long beard and being pale and haggard. Joseph was wearing a black hat with the rim down in front of his face. He was probably trying to disguise himself to avoid being recaptured.

653. Dimick Huntington took Joseph to the house where Emma was staying in Quincy. She saw him coming up the road and sprinted to meet him halfway. They spent the entire day in celebration and gratitude.

654. When Joseph took his boots off after his journey to Illinois, his feet were covered in blood.

655. Parley P. Pratt and the other prisoners in Richmond Jail, then Columbia Jail after, hopped the fence and ran away on July 4, 1839. The only prisoners who did not successfully escape were King Follet and Luman Gibbs. Luman Gibbs apostatized because of this and turned against the Church.

ILLINOIS

656. While the Prophet, First Presidency, and most other Church leaders were thrown into Missouri jails, Brigham Young and Heber C. Kimball evaded capture and jail time. The two men led the Saints to Quincy, Illinois, in early 1839. It is believed that this experience helped prepare Brigham Young for when he would lead the Saints from Illinois to Utah beginning in 1846.

657. It was a 200-mile journey (mostly on foot) from Missouri to Quincy. It took about ten traveling days to get to Quincy.

658. Emma Smith was the first in the community to be assisted in getting to Quincy. She and her children left on February 7, 1839. Stephen Markham, one of the Prophet's personal body guards, helped Emma on her journey.

659. In February 1839, the Mississippi River was frozen over. Emma, her children, their horses, and their wagon needed to cross it to get to Illinois. However, the ice was still very thin and could easily collapse under their feet. To evenly distribute the weight as much as possible, Emma had one horse walk ahead of them on the ice and pull the wagon and one horse behind them. The horses did not carry any people just in case. Emma walked across the river holding Frederick (two and a half years old) in one arm and Alexander (eight months old) in the other, while Joseph III (six years old) and Julia (seven years old) held tightly to her skirt. Miraculously, they crossed safely. They arrived in Quincy on February 15, 1839.

> EMMA SEWED THE PAGES OF THE JOSEPH SMITH TRANSLATION OF THE BIBLE TO HER SKIRT TO PROTECT THEM.

660. Emma Smith knew how important the Joseph Smith Translation of the Holy Bible was. She sewed the papers of the manuscript to the inside

of her skirt to make sure they were kept safe while she and her family journeyed to Illinois.

661. The Saints had to journey to Quincy during the cold winter because they needed to get settled in Illinois in time for spring, when they could farm crops.

662. The people in Quincy were very kind and generous to the Saints because Illinois was an abolitionist (free) state. Since Missouri was a slave state and treated the Mormons terribly, Illinois was generally happy to receive them, even if it was just to spite Missouri.

663. General John B. Clark of the Missouri militia ordered the Saints not to gather in one location again, because he thought if the Saints were spread out, then the Mormon Church would die off. The Saints were terrified of the consequences of gathering again, and rightfully so after everything they endured in Missouri. Once most of the Saints were out of Missouri, before Joseph was released from jail, they did not know if or where they were supposed to gather. The Saints were very spread out. They lived in eleven different counties. However, Brigham Young told the Saints that they needed to gather and that when Joseph Smith returned, he would tell them where to gather. He did.

664. The day after Joseph Smith's arrival, he held a council with the brethren regarding the location where the Saints would gather and settle. Only three days following Joseph's arrival in Quincy, he and Emma moved only a few miles north to Commerce to begin settling there.

665. On April 25, 1839, the Prophet Joseph Smith designated the city of Commerce as the gathering place of the Saints for the time being. Commerce would later become the city of Nauvoo.

. . . .
Nauvoo
. . . .

666. The Lord commanded the Saints to gather and build the city of Nauvoo, which was first named Commerce.

667. Before the Saints got there, only about one hundred people lived in Commerce, Illinois. They fit in well with the arriving Mormon settlers and got along well, at least at first.

668. Joseph Smith purchased some property in Commerce from Hugh White and Dr. Isaac Galland. At the time, there was only one stone house, three frame houses, and two block houses in the entire city. There were three log houses in the whole city, including the homestead owned by William White, where Joseph and Emma lived temporarily.

669. The land owner in Commerce, Dr. Isaac Galland, was baptized by Joseph Smith a few months later on July 3, 1839.

670. The rest of Commerce was destitute. The land was mostly covered with trees and bushes. The area was so wet that it was so difficult for even one person to walk through, let alone big groups of people with wagons and horses.

671. The Church eventually bought the entire peninsula in Illinois surrounded by the Mississippi River, except about 125 square feet. Nauvoo became the second-largest city in Illinois, after Chicago.

672. The Saints in Commerce who had more money and could pay more for their lot did pay more. Those who were widowed or otherwise unable to pay more paid only a small fee or sometimes even received a free lot from the Church.

673. At first it seemed like not a lot of people could live there. Nonetheless, the Saints built it up into a beautiful city called Nauvoo. In fact, Joseph Smith chose the name "Nauvoo" because it is the Hebrew word for "city beautiful," or "beautiful place."

JOSEPH AND EMMA TOOK ALL OF THE SICK INTO THEIR HOUSE AND SURROUNDING PROPERTY AND CARED FOR THEM.

674. Before enough houses were built for the Saints, sickness struck and incapacitated many in the area. Joseph and Emma took care of all the sick people and let them stay in their house. Those who were not sick stayed in tents outside Joseph and Emma's house and helped care for the sick during the day or helped build homes.

675. Nauvoo was a mostly peaceful refuge for the Saints. However, Joseph was frequently in danger of mob violence and spent a lot of time in hiding.

676. Emma Smith wrote several letters to the Illinois governor for assistance regarding Joseph's wrongful arrests and persecutions. The governor offered some assistance in response to her letters, but ultimately not enough protection for the Prophet.

677. On average, there were approximately sixteen boats docking at Nauvoo every day with new arrivals and settlers.

678. Joseph Smith knew that Nauvoo was a somewhat temporary place for the Saints to gather. He spoke about the Saints' permanent home in the Rocky Mountains on several occasions.

679. In the October 1840 conference, the Lord revealed through Joseph Smith that the Saints should focus on building two important buildings in Nauvoo. The first was the Nauvoo Temple, and the second was the Nauvoo House. It was also decided at the conference that the Church leaders would seek to be granted a city charter for Nauvoo.

680. They were granted the city charter for Nauvoo. The Nauvoo city charter allowed them to rename the city, elect government officials, and create municipal courts, a university, and their own militia. They were able to create laws and govern themselves.

681. The University of Nauvoo was one of the first universities in Illinois.

682. The city charter allowed the Saints in Nauvoo to form their own militia called the Nauvoo Legion. They were able to defend themselves with the militia without relying on other people who may be corrupt.

683. At one point, there were approximately 5,000 men between the ages of eighteen and forty-five in the Nauvoo Legion. Joseph Smith was the Commander in Chief.

684. Joseph considered the construction of the Nauvoo House to be just as important as the building of the Nauvoo Temple.

685. The Nauvoo House was originally designed to be a four-story-high hotel for travelers to stay in and learn about the gospel. However, the Nauvoo House was never completed past the first floor because of lack of resources and finances. The temporary solution was to instead expand the Mansion House, where Joseph and Emma lived, to include extra rooms for travelers and guests to stay and ponder on whether the Church was true.

686. As Nauvoo grew in population, it was divided into sections that were presided over by a bishop. They were called "wards." This was the first use of the term "ward" in an LDS context, and it is still used today to describe an area of Latter-day Saints presided over by a bishop. Back then though, their ward was also their voting region.

687. On September 14, 1840, Joseph Smith Sr. died in Nauvoo from sickness. As the Patriarch of the Church, on his deathbed he gave each of his

children a patriarchal blessing (back then, individuals could receive multiple patriarchal blessings).

688. Joseph Smith sometimes worried that he would not live long enough to finish the Lord's work. When Joseph Smith Sr. gave the Prophet a blessing before his death, he blessed Joseph for his calling and his children. He blessed Joseph that he would live to finish the work of the Lord. When his father said this, the Prophet cried out, "Oh! My father, shall I?" Joseph Smith Sr. replied, "Yes, you shall live to lay out the plan of all the work which God has given you to do . . ." and then he continued the blessing (Lucy Mack Smith, *The History of Joseph Smith by His Mother*, 274). Joseph did live to complete the work God called him to do.

689. During the late summer of 1843, Lucy Mack Smith fell severely ill. She stayed in Joseph and Emma's home. Emma took care of her. She never left Lucy's bedside for five nights straight. Emma worked so hard to take care of Lucy that she got sick too. Joseph took care of both of them until they fully recovered.

690. In the summer of 1841, Joseph was wrongfully arrested for murder, treason, and other crimes. The prosecutor at Joseph's trial tried hard to convict Joseph of these crimes, but his efforts were in vain. The prosecutor had only spoken for a few minutes when he vomited at the judge's feet. Needless to say, the defense won the case.

> AT JOSEPH'S TRIAL IN 1841, THE PROSECUTOR VOMITED AT THE JUDGE'S FEET AND LOST THE CASE.

691. On May 6, 1842, former governor of Missouri Lilburn W. Boggs was rumored to have been shot by an assassin. Lilburn Boggs survived the attempted murder. However, since it was Boggs's Extermination Order that caused so much persecution of the Saints in Missouri, many claimed that Joseph Smith must have been involved in the shooting. However, Joseph was hundreds of miles away at a public training in Illinois the day following the shooting. He was seen at the training by thousands of witnesses. He could not have shot the former governor.

692. When people could not prove that Joseph Smith shot former Governor Boggs, they instead said he must have ordered Orrin Porter Rockwell, one of Joseph's body guards, to shoot him. Rockwell was in Missouri at the time of the shooting but denied having any involvement with

the attempted assassination. Joseph Smith also denied having any involvement.

693. The accusers pursued both Porter Rockwell and Joseph Smith. Porter and Joseph both went into hiding. Authorities found Rockwell and arrested him. Joseph Smith eventually surrendered and voluntarily went to Springfield for his trial. He was tried for accessory to attempted murder on Lilburn W. Boggs. The judge, Nathaniel Pope, found the case against Joseph to be ridiculous, and Joseph was acquitted and sent home. Rockwell's trial ended in his release as well.

694. Apostates and anti-Mormons have since claimed that Joseph Smith admitted to them that he sent Orrin Porter Rockwell to kill Lilburn Boggs. It is important to note that these people strongly hated Joseph Smith. The men who accused him of admitting his involvement in this crime were the same men who later conspired to kill Joseph Smith at Carthage Jail. Those who were faithful to the Church, and those who were closest to the Prophet—his family, wife, and closest friends—never claimed he had any involvement or ever admitted to such things.

695. Whenever Joseph Smith was in hiding, he always had a friend to accompany him. While he was avoiding arrest for the crime of accessory to the attempted murder of former Governor Boggs, he had John Taylor with him. Before they left, John Taylor was so sick that he could not even stand up. Joseph told him that if he would go with him, he would feel good the entire journey. John Taylor went with Joseph Smith and was healed.

JOSEPH SMITH WAS APPOINTED MAYOR OF NAUVOO ON MAY 19, 1842.

696. On May 19, 1842, Joseph Smith was appointed mayor of Nauvoo at the Nauvoo City Council.

697. Joseph Smith was also voted to the office of Lieutenant General, Commander in Chief, of the Nauvoo Legion.

698. In January 1841, Joseph Smith received the revelation that the Church needed to fill the whole earth. He called the first international missionaries to go on missions to the United Kingdom. These twelve men actually belonged to the Quorum of the Twelve Apostles of the Church.

699. One day Wilford Woodruff taught 600 members of a church called the United Brethren in the Gadfield Elm Chapel in England. He converted 599 people to The Church of Jesus Christ of Latter-day Saints that day. The Gadfield Elm Chapel was originally owned by the United Brethren but was deeded to the Mormon Church afterwards. It is the first international Church historic site, as well as the very first chapel owned by The Church of Jesus Christ of Latter-day Saints.

700. It is believed that the mission of the Twelve to the UK was what helped prepare them to lead the Church after Joseph's death.

701. The first LDS missionary to teach in a foreign language was a man named Addison Pratt in 1844. He spent some of his life in Honolulu, so when Joseph called him to be a missionary, he was able to preach to the Polynesians in their native languages before Hawaii became a state. He later went to spread the gospel in the Pacific Islands, the Austral Islands, and Tahiti.

THE NAUVOO TEMPLE

702. The Nauvoo Temple was not only the spiritual center of Nauvoo, it was also the geographical center of Nauvoo. The Nauvoo Temple is located one mile south of the northern shore, one mile north of the southern shore, and one mile west of the eastern shore, placing it in the exact center of the peninsula.

703. To find the right architect for the job, Joseph Smith had the designers send him their ideas for the Nauvoo Temple, and Joseph's favorite submission would win.

704. Joseph Smith chose William Weeks to be the architect of the Nauvoo Temple.

705. During the blueprinting stages of the Nauvoo Temple, the temple was designed with only rectangular-shaped windows. One day, Joseph came to William Weeks and said he saw a vision of the Nauvoo Temple and that it had both rectangular windows and round windows on the side. He told Weeks to change the entire plan to make sure the temple had round windows. There are both rectangular and round windows on the side of the Nauvoo Temple.

706. Joseph Smith instructed William Weeks to build the basement of the temple deep enough for a baptismal font, so they could perform baptisms for the dead. They were not able to perform baptisms for the dead in the Kirtland Temple, so this was especially exciting and important.

707. William Weeks built the baptismal font in the basement of the Nauvoo Temple in a similar manner in which they are built today. The font rested on the backs of twelve oxen, with the same symbolic meanings they have today.

708. The Saints dedicated one day out of every ten days (not counting Sundays) to help work on the Nauvoo Temple. At this point, Nauvoo was divided into ten wards. Each ward was assigned one day to work on the temple, and then ten days later they would work on their assigned day again; it would continue this way until it was finished.

709. Originally, the plan was to build a tabernacle in front of the Nauvoo Temple. It never became a reality, because most of the Saints had to leave Nauvoo before they could start building the tabernacle.

710. Joseph Smith taught that every individual would hear the gospel and have the choice to accept it. If they do not receive the gospel in this life, then their ordinances would be completed in temples for them by proxy.

711. In September 1843, Emma Smith was the first woman to receive her endowment. Joseph instructed her how to officiate temple ordinances for other women. She did so until shortly before Joseph's death. Emma Smith was the only woman in this dispensation to be given authority to officiate temple ordinances from the Prophet Joseph Smith himself.

JOSEPH DIED BEFORE THE NAUVOO TEMPLE WAS COMPLETED.

712. Joseph Smith died before the Nauvoo Temple was completed. However, Joseph did still finish his work of restoring all sacred temple ordinances before his death. All temple ordinances—baptisms, endowments, sealings, and so forth—were performed in other sacred locations with only worthy Church members present before the temple was completed and dedicated. They were usually performed in the room on the second floor of the Red Brick Store, where the Relief Society was formed.

713. The Lord allowed this to occur only in early Nauvoo before the temple was finished so Joseph could finish the work of fully restoring the gospel

before his death. Now that temples are available in locations all over the world, these sacred ordinances are not to be performed anywhere else besides inside the temple, by those authorized to do so by God. They are sacred ordinances to be performed only in sacred places anointed by God.

FORMATION OF THE
RELIEF SOCIETY

714. During the construction of the Nauvoo Temple, a woman named Sarah Granger Kimball formed the "Sewing Society." It was a society of women who made clothes for the men working on the Nauvoo Temple. Forming a society like this was not uncommon.

715. These societies would form constitutions by which they would abide. Sarah Granger Kimball asked Eliza R. Snow to write the constitution for the Sewing Society. Eliza wrote the constitution and showed it to Joseph Smith. Joseph loved it.

716. It was the Sewing Society for the Nauvoo Temple's constitution that inspired Joseph Smith's revelation that the Lord wanted the women to form a society in the Church. It was originally called the Female Relief Society of Nauvoo. Today, it is simply called the Relief Society.

717. Joseph Smith organized the Relief Society on March 17, 1842. The first meeting was held on this date on the second floor of the Red Brick Store in Nauvoo.

718. All adult women in The Church of Jesus Christ of Latter-day Saints are members of Relief Society.

719. Joseph Smith revealed that God wanted the Priesthood and the Relief Society to complement each other. They are equal in the eyes of God and the Church.

720. The Prophet taught that the Church was never completely restored until the Relief Society was organized. Not much is known about the organization of women in Christ's original church; it is not discussed often in the New Testament. However, the evidence demonstrates that women members were essential to Christ's church and ministry.

Therefore, the Relief Society needed to be organized for the fulness of the gospel to be perfectly restored.

721. Joseph Smith sometimes taught the women in Relief Society. He taught them to love each other and work in harmony as one unit to help others in need.

722. The women loved and adored Joseph Smith. He did not get to teach the women in Relief Society often because he was so busy. Whenever he did teach in Relief Society, the women who wrote about it spoke of those lessons as beloved, precious treasures.

723. Contrary to some modern belief, the organization of the Relief Society was way ahead of its time in the nineteenth century. In the traditional religious culture of the 1800s, women were not to have callings or leadership positions at all and were to be silent in church. This was another element of The Church of Jesus Christ of Latter-day Saints that differed from the other religious sects of that time.

724. Who was the very first Relief Society president, and how was she called to this position? All the adult women in the Church, comprising the Relief Society, voted Emma Smith to be the first Relief Society president. President Emma Smith called Elizabeth Ann Whitney and Sarah M. Cleveland as her counselors.

JOSEPH SMITH FOR PRESIDENT

725. In 1833, before Joseph Smith even moved to Missouri, the Saints in that state suffered intense persecution. When their land and possessions were stolen by the mob, Joseph felt that the Saints' rights had been violated. Years later, Joseph Smith went to Washington, DC, to speak to the president of the United States and to Congress, seeking financial assistance for the Saints.

726. It took about a month for Joseph and the others to reach Washington, DC, from Nauvoo. The quest was in vain. They were denied.

727. Joseph and a few other Church leaders once spoke with President Martin Van Buren to seek assistance against the Missouri persecution. The president responded that he would lose the vote of Missouri in the next election if he took action, and he refused to help them.

728. Joseph Smith later wrote saying that President Martin Van Buren actually left the room mid-conversation with the Church leaders, never to return. The Saints had no choice but to leave disappointed.

729. The Saints demanded an appeal to President Van Buren's decision. Van Buren did reconsider his decision against helping the Church but ultimately did not change his stance. This broke Joseph Smith's heart because he voted for Martin Van Buren in the election but now felt betrayed by him. Joseph started speaking out against the president, especially among the Saints, and did not vote for him again in the next election.

730. An interesting, little-known aspect of this story is that whenever Joseph introduced himself to the political leaders in Washington, DC, during this trip, he only claimed to be a member of the LDS Church. He did not introduce himself as the "Prophet," "President of the Church," "First Elder," etc. He was only going to seek assistance, not to use his influential position in the Church as leverage or to intimidate.

731. After much more persecution in Missouri, leading to the Mormon exodus from the state, and then more denial of any assistance from the government, Joseph Smith decided that he should run for president of the United States. Joseph Smith had other motives for running for president as well. It would give the Saints a presidential candidate that they could trust fully. It would not only raise awareness of The Church of Jesus Christ of Latter-day Saints, but also raise awareness of their sufferings and mistreatments.

JOSEPH SMITH ANNOUNCED HIS CANDIDACY FOR PRESIDENT OF THE UNITED STATES OF AMERICA IN 1844.

732. Joseph Smith announced his candidacy for the president of the United States of America at the Mansion Home in Nauvoo in early 1844.

733. Sidney Rigdon was running with Joseph Smith Jr. for the position of vice president.

734. During the time of Joseph Smith's presidential campaign, the most important national issues involved slavery, states' rights, and whether the United States should grow to extend from the Atlantic Ocean to the Pacific Ocean.

735. Joseph Smith's platform was that he would reduce Congress and their salaries, abolish slavery, give more authority to the federal government than the state governments, and annex California, Oregon, and Texas. He also wanted to reform prisons. He believed that prisons should not be only about punishment, but should be more like rehabilitation facilities where prisoners can take classes, educate themselves, and become better people. His views were very progressive for that time, and generally became reality for the country in the years following.

736. It is not clear how likely it was that Joseph Smith would have won the presidency. Historian and author Richard Lyman Bushman suggests the possibility that Joseph Smith started his campaign as a person for those who did not like the other candidates to vote for. Bushman believes it was more of a protest than a serious candidacy, until his campaign started to gain traction and a following. Then, Joseph Smith could have genuinely had a chance at winning. Joseph died before the election.

737. Presidential campaigns back then were not as time consuming and stressful as they are today. When Joseph Smith ran for president, he and the Quorum of the Twelve supervised over 300 missionaries who would go out and teach the gospel, as well as spread the word about Joseph's candidacy.

> JOSEPH SMITH WAS THE FIRST PRESIDENTIAL CANDIDATE IN AMERICAN HISTORY TO BE MURDERED DURING THEIR CAMPAIGN.

738. Many non-Mormons feared that Joseph Smith's presidential campaign meant that Mormons were trying to take over the world. They did not like it. This fear played a significant role in the Prophet's martyrdom.

739. Joseph Smith was the first presidential candidate in American history to be murdered during their campaign.

740. MYTH: Joseph Smith ran for president of the United States, but the Lord told him to resign because he was running against the man who was supposed to become president, Abraham Lincoln. FACT: This is a confusing and weird myth. Joseph Smith ran for President in 1844. His candidacy ended when he was killed at Carthage Jail. Abraham Lincoln was elected President on November 6, 1860, sixteen years after the Prophet's death. In fact, there is no known documentation of the two

men ever crossing paths. That does not mean that they never crossed paths at all, but it is not likely.

741. This myth probably derives from the story of when Joseph Smith prophesied to Stephen A. Douglas that Douglas would run for president of the United States but would feel God's wrath if he turned against the Church. Stephen A. Douglas did run for president of the United States and seemed like the most obvious candidate for the presidency. However, in a presidential debate, Douglas viciously slandered the Church and expressed that Congress should kick the Church out of the country. Suddenly, Stephen A. Douglas lost the presidency to an obscure non-politician named Abraham Lincoln.

JOSEPH SMITH AND FREEMASONRY

742. Freemasons are individuals who have joined the somewhat exclusive club of freemasonry in the pursuit of knowledge.

743. There are multiple levels of freemasonry that a person can achieve as they obtain more knowledge. The knowledge obtained is not religious in nature. However, freemasons are not prohibited from having their own religious beliefs outside of freemasonry.

744. Masons are usually influential and powerful people. Becoming a mason and interacting with other influential and powerful people can help build political and community influence. It is believed this was one of the reasons why Joseph Smith became a freemason, to help build influence of the Saints and reduce persecution.

745. There are certain symbols and actions that masons do that many believe Joseph Smith stole to use in the temple endowment ceremony. However, freemasonry actually derives from ancient religious rituals, even though they are not based in theology. While there are some similarities, they are not exactly connected.

746. It is possible that Joseph knew there were similarities between the two kinds of rituals before he was initiated into freemasonry. Therefore, he may have joined so he could learn how to better introduce the temple endowment ceremony rituals.

747. The first five Presidents of The Church of Jesus Christ of Latter-day Saints were freemasons: Joseph Smith, Brigham Young, John Taylor, Wilford Woodruff, and Lorenzo Snow. Walt Disney, Mozart, Napoleon, and over a dozen presidents of the United States were also freemasons.

JOSEPH SMITH AND PLURAL MARRIAGE

748. Hyrum Smith's first wife, Jerusha, died on October 13, 1837. She left behind five small children. Hyrum was heartbroken and distraught. Joseph told Hyrum not to worry about her salvation and revealed that she would rise again on the morning of the first resurrection.

749. On July 12, 1843, Joseph Smith dictated the revelation on eternal marriage (including plural marriage) to Hyrum Smith and William Clayton. William Clayton wrote the revelation in Joseph's journal. Hyrum Smith requested that the revelation be written down so the message could be easier explained.

750. The revelation came from God as a result of Joseph's question regarding why God allowed certain men in Biblical times, like David, Abraham, and Solomon, to have many wives and concubines. It really bothered Joseph and confused him for years. The Lord answered that He gave those specific, worthy men multiple wives and concubines to help grow their seed of good children, whom would be righteously taught and led back to Heavenly Father because they were born of righteous parents.

751. The Lord commanded that Joseph Smith and a few select Church leaders, with their wives' and future wives' consent, to begin practicing plural marriage as well.

752. The revelation came as a huge shock and trial of faith for every member of the Church who heard it. Joseph Smith was no exception. In fact, he resisted and strongly tried to avoid practicing plural marriage or teaching it to the Saints. The practice was not widely known in the Church until the Saints settled in Utah under the presidency of Brigham Young.

753. The revelation states that a man (or woman) cannot be exalted (reside in the highest place in the celestial kingdom) without being sealed to his or her spouse in the temple by the proper priesthood authority.

754. Marriages—plural or monogamous—performed in the temple by somebody given the priesthood authority to do so, last for time and all eternity. Marriages—plural or monogamous—not performed in the temple, end at death. Those who were never married, or were married outside of the temple and the sealing ordinance was never performed, are not exalted with their spouses. At death, they become single and separate angels who cannot live in the highest realm of the celestial kingdom or live eternally with their spouses.

> MARRIAGES PERFORMED IN THE TEMPLE LAST FOR TIME AND ALL ETERNITY.

755. After they die though, sealings can still be performed for them and their spouse in temples on earth by proxy of those who are still living. Then they can be exalted and live with their spouse eternally. If they were never married in life, they can have the opportunity to be sealed to somebody in heaven. Sometimes the person we are supposed to spend eternity with is somebody we never met in our lifetime.

756. Arguably the best example to increase understanding of the justification and reasoning behind plural marriage in the early days of the Church is the story of the marriage between Hyrum Smith and Mercy Thompson.

757. Mercy Thompson, Robert Thompson's wife, was Joseph Smith's private secretary and one of the editors of the *Times and Seasons* newspaper. Robert seemed perfectly healthy when he unexpectedly died in the fall of 1841. He died at thirty years old, leaving behind his wife and their three-year-old daughter. Random deaths from disease and accident were very common in those days. Back then, women had limited rights. They were usually not able to own property, hold a real job, vote, run for office, etc. If a woman's husband died and she did not remarry soon, she could expect a life of extreme poverty or even death of herself and her children within a few years.

758. Hyrum Smith was married to Mercy's sister, Mary Fielding Smith, at this time. He married Mary after his first wife, Jerusha, passed away during childbirth. Mary and Hyrum shared a sweet marriage of love and affection until his death in 1844. Mary took care of Jerusha's children like they were her own. The two families were very close. Mercy and

Robert helped take care of Mary and Hyrum's children during Hyrum's incarceration in Liberty Jail. In Nauvoo, the two families built homes next to each other.

759. After her husband's death, Mercy found solace in the company of her sister Mary. One night, Mercy was staying with Mary while Hyrum was out on business. Mercy had a dream that she knew was a message from God. She dreamt that she was standing in a beautiful garden with Robert. She heard an unknown voice repeating their marriage vows. She woke up elated. That night, Hyrum had a very similar dream from God while he was away from home. He dreamt of his deceased wife, Jerusha, and their two children who had also passed away. The timing of their mirroring dreams was no coincidence.

760. When Hyrum returned home, Joseph told him about the revelation on eternal marriage. Marriages not contracted for time and all eternity ended at death unless a new contract was made for time and all eternity. Hyrum wondered how he could possibly be sealed to Jerusha since she was dead. Joseph revealed that a living person could stand in as a proxy for the deceased person during the sealing ceremony. This new revelation on eternal marriage thrilled Mercy Thompson. She knew she would be reunited with Robert after death and live with him forever.

761. One morning in late May 1843, Mercy Thompson, Mary Fielding Smith, and Hyrum and Joseph Smith met in a room in Joseph's house. Joseph sealed Mercy to her deceased husband Robert for time and all eternity, Hyrum stood as the proxy for Robert. Joseph also sealed Mary Smith and Hyrum for time and all eternity. Finally, Joseph sealed Hyrum to his dead wife, Jerusha, for time and all eternity, and his wife Mary stood as proxy for Jerusha. It was a joyous and beautiful ceremony.

762. Mercy Thompson was ecstatic to know she would be with her husband again for eternity. However, she was still a widow in a time when single women struggled to survive. That summer, Joseph was visited by an angel. The angel was Robert Thompson, Mercy Thompson's dead husband. He requested that Joseph have Hyrum be sealed to Mercy for time (only during life). Mercy and Robert would still be sealed eternally. However, Hyrum would have the obligation and responsibility of taking care of Mercy and her daughter until his death.

763. Joseph was seriously reluctant to enter into plural marriages at first. It was illegal in the United States and would bring much more heavy persecution on the Church. An angel visited Joseph three times, urging

him to move forward as the Lord commanded. The angel threatened Joseph with destruction and even carried a flaming sword of fire. Even then, Joseph was still afraid and cautious.

> JOSEPH WAS VERY RELUCTANT TO ENTER INTO PLURAL MARRIAGES AT FIRST, EVEN AFTER AN ANGEL VISITED HIM THREE TIMES, URGING HIM TO MOVE FORWARD.

764. Both Mercy Thompson and Hyrum Smith were strongly opposed to the idea of plural marriage as well. Hyrum eventually agreed with plural marriage when he realized he wanted to be with both Mary and Jerusha for time and all eternity. He never wanted to part with either of them, even though Mary had to gain her own testimony of it as well. Mary Fielding Smith was arguably more excited about Hyrum marrying her sister than even Hyrum and Mercy were. She was delighted to be closer to her sister, while also knowing Mercy would be taken care of.

765. Mercy Thompson prayed long and hard for many days about this new revelation. After speaking with the Prophet regarding his experience seeing her husband, she gained testimony that it was from God and that it was necessary. She knew her husband really came and requested Joseph to speak to Hyrum about it. Joseph also prayed to confirm that the message was actually from God before he spoke with Hyrum. Mercy was only going to be married to Hyrum until he would deliver her to Robert when they were resurrected.

766. Like Mercy Thompson, other Latter-day Saint women who were converted to the principal of plural marriage often wrote about glorious spiritual experiences confirming its truthfulness and purity. Some saw lights, heard voices, and even saw angels. This was not a misogynistic, slimy way for Church leaders to marry several women (despite some who unfortunately did live the practice immorally). It was a God-sanctioned way to help take care of Latter-day Saint women and their children.

767. Nobody, man or woman, easily accepted plural marriage. Every person had to receive their own witness and testimony of its importance before accepting it.

768. Upon initially hearing the revelation on plural marriage from Joseph Smith, William Law cried and begged Joseph not to teach it. Joseph said he had no choice because God threatened to destroy the Prophet if he did not obey and ask others to obey as well. William Law was later

ironically excommunicated for adultery. He became bitter and had a huge influence in Joseph Smith's eventual murder.

769. On August 11, 1843, Joseph married Hyrum and Mercy Thompson. The ceremony was performed in Hyrum and Mary's home. Joseph recommended that Hyrum build an additional room to their house where Mercy could live. He did so. Hyrum took care of Mercy financially until his death in 1844. Mercy adored Hyrum. She mourned Hyrum's death. She was so grateful to Hyrum for all he had done for her, but she lived for the reunion with Robert Thompson. In 1846, Mary, Mercy, and their brother left with Brigham Young's group to Salt Lake City. They lived the rest of their lives there together. After Mary's death, Mercy cared for the children that Mary and Hyrum had left behind. She died in 1893, still retaining the name Mercy R. Thompson.

770. The revelation on eternal marriage, found in Doctrine and Covenants 132, was not written down until the year 1843. However, evidence suggests that Joseph Smith received the revelation as early as 1831. There is evidence to support that Joseph married his first plural wife in early 1833. Her name was Fanny Alger. She was a housemaid in Joseph and Emma's home.

771. Emma Smith really struggled with the revelation on plural marriage. Women who were close to Emma said that she knew it was a commandment from God and that Joseph did not imagine it or fabricate it for selfish reasons. Nonetheless, it was probably one of her most difficult trials to endure. She would be accepting of plural marriage one day and be completely supportive, and the next day she would have an extremely difficult time accepting it again.

772. In fact, Hyrum suggested that a copy of the original revelation on plural marriage be carefully copied by Joseph Kingsbury just in case. An identical copy was made. Shortly after, Emma Smith destroyed the original.

773. Joseph Smith was sealed to some women who were already married to other men. As disturbing and weird as that sounds, it actually makes more sense when understanding the context and reasoning. Joseph Smith was sealed to women whose husbands were not worthy of being sealed to them in the temple for time and all eternity. It is

JOSEPH WAS SEALED TO WOMEN WHOSE HUSBANDS WERE NOT WORTHY OF BEING SEALED TO THEM FOR ETERNITY.

unfair for a righteous woman and her children to be disqualified from exaltation based solely on the actions of her husband. Instead, they were sealed to the Prophet.

774. Another reason behind this is the fact that children born to these women would not have fathers that were worthy to be sealed to them in the temple. Even though none of these kids were Joseph Smith's children biologically, they are still sealed to him through their mother. Some of the husbands even consented to their wives being sealed to the Prophet.

775. Nobody knows exactly how many plural wives Joseph Smith had during his lifetime. Historians and scholars generally agree that he likely married a little over thirty women.

776. It is not clear whether or not Joseph Smith had any sexual relationships with his plural wives. There are several accounts, especially from apostates like William Law and William McLellin, suggesting that Joseph Smith did have sexual relations with other women besides Emma. Some women have even claimed that Joseph Smith is the actual father of their children. However, modern DNA technology has proven all of those claims to be false. Joseph and Emma together had eleven children. To think that Joseph Smith were sexually involved with thirty other women but had no babies with any of them, in a time before birth control, seems silly and illogical. However, there is no way to prove whether he did or did not.

777. Other Church leaders who practiced plural marriage, including Brigham Young, did have sexual relations with their plural wives. It seems like it was probably decided between each husband, first wife, and each individual plural wife whether sexual relations would be involved. Again, there is no way to know how the decisions were made in each individual circumstance.

778. Plural marriage was only authorized and practiced by a small percentage of Church leadership, not the entire Church. It was mostly kept secret to avoid mob violence and more persecution on the Saints until they found safe refuge in Salt Lake City, Utah. The practice was discontinued in 1890 under the direction of Prophet Wilford Woodruff. Utah was about to become a state in the US, and polygamy is illegal in the United States. Some chose to continue the practice and were excommunicated. Some even created their own sect that allowed them to continue practicing polygamy. Several of these religious sects still exist today.

JOSEPH SMITH'S LAST MONTHS

779.   In March 1844, Joseph Smith held a meeting with the Quorum of the Twelve Apostles in which he instructed them on how to lead the Church. This meeting came to be known as Joseph Smith's "Last Charge."

780.   Joseph Smith told the Twelve during the "Last Charge" that he was growing tired and worn out from the burden of leading the Church and looked forward to his rest.

781.   In the "Last Charge" meeting, Joseph stated that God was urging him to bestow the priesthood keys and power of leading the Church upon the Twelve. Joseph said he believed it could be because his enemies were about to take his life. If Joseph were to die without bestowing the keys on the Twelve, then the keys of the one true church would be lost again forever.

782.   In this meeting, Joseph told the Twelve that it was their responsibility to lead the Church after Joseph Smith died.

783.   Those in attendance of the meeting wrote that Joseph seemed joyful and peaceful after bestowing the keys on the brethren. It was like he was exceptionally relieved.

784.   The "Last Charge" meeting was also held to help prepare the Twelve to go out and campaign for Joseph's presidency.

785.   About two weeks later, the Twelve left to journey throughout the country to campaign for Joseph Smith.

786.   Joseph's friend King Follett died on March 9, 1844. He was killed by a falling bucket of rocks that struck him in the head while he worked on a well.

787.   On April 7, 1844, a general conference was held shortly after King Follett's funeral. Joseph Smith spoke at the conference about "the subject of the dead," in light of the recent death of King Follett. Today,

his speech is referred to as the "King Follett Discourse" or the "King Follett Sermon." The conference was attended by more than 20,000 people.

788. The King Follett discourse is arguably Joseph Smith's most famous and notable speech. Literary scholars and critics—Mormon and non-Mormon alike—have named it among one of the most remarkable speeches in American history. It was given only less than three months before the Prophet's death.

JOSEPH'S KING FOLLET SERMON HAS NOT BEEN CANONIZED INTO LATTER-DAY SAINT DOCTRINE.

789. A full account of the speech was not completely documented at the time. However, Thomas Bullock gathered several accounts of the speech, along with notes from those in attendance, to compose what is believed to be almost the entire speech. It was published in 1971 in the April issue of the *Ensign* magazine. The speech has not been canonized as one of the standard works of the LDS Church.

790. In the King Follett Sermon, Joseph Smith revealed new doctrinal topics. He spoke about the existence of God and God's creations having no beginning, that we, as intelligences, existed before God formed us as His spirit children and then sent us to Earth to get a body and be tested. He used the analogy of eternity being like his wedding ring, with no beginning or end.

791. He spoke about the first principle of the gospel of Jesus Christ to know the character of God and that we can speak with God ourselves and receive revelation from Him. While speaking about the character and nature of God, Joseph revealed that God was once like we are, and then He became exalted and became God.

792. Joseph Smith also stated that as God was once like we are now, we can someday become like Him. It is not exactly clear what Joseph Smith meant by this. It is often assumed or believed that Joseph was saying that righteous members of the Church will one day be able to become Gods themselves and create their own worlds and beings. There is not exactly proof that this is what Joseph Smith meant. It is not considered Church doctrine, at least not at this point in time. That is likely why

this speech has not been canonized, because it is not exactly clear what the Prophet was trying to say on this matter specifically.

793. Joseph Smith also revealed in this speech that all men and women can be saved through Christ's Atonement and through repentance, whether in this mortal life or after death, unless they have committed the unpardonable sin. The unpardonable sin that Joseph Smith was referring to is denying the Holy Ghost. To deny the Holy Ghost, somebody would have to see Jesus Christ and/or the Holy Ghost and then deny their existence completely. It is not just denying a testimony, to commit the unpardonable sin, but that a person must *know*. For example, Joseph Smith saw and spoke with Heavenly Father and Jesus Christ several times. If he ever denied his experiences or their existence, he would have committed the unpardonable sin and would never be able to repent for that. Besides the unpardonable sin, the atonement allows us to repent for anything and everything. That is an amazing blessing, something we will probably never fully understand in this life.

794. Since Joseph had so often barely escaped death before, some of the Saints started to believe that Joseph was somehow immortal. Joseph had to explain that this belief was false and that Joseph was able to die at any time once the work was finished.

795. In the later years of Nauvoo, Joseph Smith sometimes expressed his feelings that his life would soon come to an end.

796. Brigham Young wrote that he once heard Joseph say that he would not live to the age of forty. Brigham believed that his own faith could somehow prevent Joseph's death, but that was not Heavenly Father's plan. Joseph Smith died at the age of thirty-eight.

797. A woman named Elizabeth Rollins wrote in her journal that the Prophet once told her that he believed the Lord would require that he seal his testimony with his own blood. To prove to the world that Joseph Smith really believed the Book of Mormon and the teachings of the Church he founded, he would need to die for the cause.

JOSEPH ONCE TOLD ELIZABETH ROLLINS THAT HE BELIEVED THE LORD WOULD REQUIRE THAT HE SEAL HIS TESTIMONY WITH HIS OWN BLOOD.

798. Joseph Smith actually knew the struggles and trials the Saints would have to endure after

his death on their trek to Utah. Just a short while before his death, he spoke to a friend about how blessed and amazing the Saints of Nauvoo were. Then he alluded to their obliviousness of the trials that awaited them.

799. During this time, some former members of the Church were renouncing the gospel and the Prophet. They claimed Joseph must have been a "fallen prophet" because he was not receiving as much revelation as he did in the early years of the Church. The revelation on plural marriage might have influenced their new opinions of Joseph as well. Many of these people were those who conspired to kill Joseph Smith.

800. Joseph Smith, as mayor of Nauvoo, was organizing the state police force when he alluded to having an enemy similar to Brutus plotting to kill him, and that Joseph would probably survive longer if it weren't for him. Joseph was just speaking of his enemies in general, but some people thought he was referring to William Law. They told William, which caused him to fear for his life and seek vengeance. Joseph immediately held a counsel to clear the air, but it was no use. William Law had already begun to plot the murder of Joseph Smith.

801. In Ramus, Illinois, a group of apostates intentionally committed theft so they could be arrested. When asked why they committed the crimes, they claimed that Joseph Smith told the Mormons that stealing was allowed, if the victims were Gentiles. They lied in an attempt to increase disdain for Joseph Smith and the Mormons in Illinois.

802. After this, rumors spread that the Nauvoo Mormons were responsible for all the crimes committed in Illinois and that Joseph Smith was encouraging the unlawful acts. This was also completely untrue.

803. Since Joseph Smith had so often been arrested and then later acquitted, non-Mormons in Illinois began to view the Prophet as a manipulator of the law who could get himself acquitted even if he was guilty. It was not true. He was acquitted because he was innocent. Regardless, the increasing negative public opinion of Joseph Smith led even more people to plan his demise.

804. Thomas Sharp, a non-Mormon in Illinois, created a newspaper called *The Warsaw Signal*. It often spoke about the Church. At first, its contents were seemingly unbiased and did not speak negatively about the Church or Joseph Smith. However, one article was released that Joseph Smith

thought portrayed him and the Church in a negative light. He wrote a sour letter to Thomas Sharp about it.

805. Thomas Sharp was deeply offended by the intense response from the Prophet. After that, Thomas Sharp's articles became vindictive and hateful toward Joseph Smith and the Mormons. His articles only increased the hatred toward the Saints. *The Warsaw Signal* became one of the most vocal and powerful voices against the Prophet Joseph Smith.

806. In an attempt to have more political influence against the Saints, Thomas Sharp created the anti-Mormon political party. They were not violent against the Saints, at least at first. They lost the 1841 and 1842 elections.

807. A man named Joseph Jackson wished to marry Hyrum's oldest daughter, Lovina. He asked Hyrum for permission but was rejected. Jackson then went to Joseph Smith and asked him to persuade Hyrum. Joseph refused. Joseph and Hyrum apparently thought Jackson was not a good person to marry Lovina, and rightfully so. Joseph Jackson became enraged. He went to William Law and several more of Joseph's enemies. They joined together and plotted to murder the entire Smith family.

808. Joseph Jackson would hold secret meetings with the Higbees, Laws, and Fosters (Dr. Foster was the justice of the peace) and conspire against the Smith family. Eventually they established a printing press to express and spread their hatred. It was called the *Nauvoo Expositor*.

THE NAUVOO EXPOSITOR

809. The *Nauvoo Expositor* was established in June 1844, only a few weeks before Joseph and Hyrum's deaths.

810. The *Nauvoo Expositor* was created with the intention of arousing the public against the Mormons, and especially against Joseph Smith.

811. The *Nauvoo Expositor* only published one issue before it was destroyed. It was four pages long.

812. Contrary to popular modern understanding, the *Nauvoo Expositor* published more than just anti-Mormon content. The *Nauvoo Expositor* also shared news of recent marriages and even some poetry publications.

813. Regardless, Joseph Smith beheld a vision that the continuing publication of the *Nauvoo Expositor* would lead to more bloodshed of the Saints.

814. For the public peace, Joseph Smith and the Nauvoo Legion swiftly and quietly burned down the printing press of the *Nauvoo Expositor*. It sounds crazy and uncalled for, and today it would be considered both. However, the freedom of press was not considered to be applicable to each state yet. Burning down the printing press for the *Nauvoo Expositor* was totally legal at the time. That is not to say that it was necessarily the right thing to do, but it was legal and handled relatively professionally.

> JOSEPH AND THE NAUVOO LEGION BURNED DOWN THE PRINTING PRESS OF THE *NAUVOO EXPOSITOR*.

815. All the families behind the *Nauvoo Expositor* publication were angry and left Nauvoo for a nearby city named Carthage. They swore vengeance on Joseph Smith, the Nauvoo City Council, and the entire city of Nauvoo.

816. They tried to get Joseph arrested but were mostly unsuccessful. They then went to Colonel Levi Williams, commander of a militia and one of the Church's enemies. Colonel Williams went to Governor Thomas Ford for assistance.

817. The tension grew intense. Governor Thomas Ford requested that Joseph and Hyrum Smith voluntarily go to Carthage for trial or he would send a militia into Nauvoo, which would likely mean the loss of many lives. If they did go to Carthage, he promised them protection from mob violence.

818. Joseph and Hyrum at first tried avoiding going to Carthage. On June 24, 1844, Joseph rode a ferry across the river to Iowa. They were only on the island a short time when some in Nauvoo sent a messenger to Joseph who called him a coward for running away. It broke his heart and they went back to Nauvoo.

819. Brigham Young later said he believed that if the Twelve were still in Nauvoo at the time, they would never have allowed Joseph to come back to Nauvoo from Iowa. They would have tried to protect him. He believed Joseph and Hyrum would have lived if the Twelve were there to help.

820. That night, Hyrum and Joseph spent a wonderful and peaceful night with their families in the Mansion Home.

821. The family had good reason to celebrate. Hyrum performed the wedding of his oldest daughter, Lovina, to a man named Lorin Walker, and they held a small celebration in the home that night.

822. Mary Fielding Smith and Emma Hale Smith did not seem too deeply concerned when their husbands left for Carthage Jail. They had always come home safely before, and they believed they would safely return once more.

823. Before Joseph left for Carthage, Emma asked him to give her a blessing. There was sadly not enough time. Joseph told her that instead she should write out her own blessing of whatever she wanted and then Joseph would sign it for her. She did so, but unfortunately, Joseph never returned from Carthage to sign it for her. In the blessing, she wrote that she desired to receive daily wisdom from Heavenly Father, to understand herself, to be able to raise her children to be instruments in God's kingdom, to live with a cheerful countenance and finish the work she needed to do on earth, and to be able to see God's hands in every part of her life.

824. When Joseph left for Carthage, Emma and Joseph had four kids ranging from ages six to thirteen. She was also four months pregnant with David Hyrum Smith. He was born after the Prophet's death.

825. Joseph and Hyrum left for Carthage, Illinois, early on the morning of June 24, 1844.

826. After leaving his wife and children the first time, Joseph came back to see Emma again for a few minutes. He begged her to come with him. She refused because she was pregnant and sick with chills and fever.

827. On their way, Joseph said to Hyrum, "I am going like a lamb to the slaughter; but I am calm as a summer's morning; I have a conscience void of offense towards God, and towards all men. I shall die innocent, and it shall yet be said of me—he was murdered in cold blood" (Doctrine and Covenants 135:4).

828. Several Church leaders in the Nauvoo City Council had a warrant out for their arrest in Carthage. On June 24, 1844, they went to Carthage for their hearing. They were all let go. The judge ruled that Joseph and Hyrum would be given bail for $10,000.

829. Stephen Markham heard that Joseph and Hyrum could be released on bail. He immediately sold his home, putting his family in a tent. Joseph and Hyrum were released. It was all in vain.

CARTHAGE JAIL AND THE MARTYRDOMS

830. On the morning of June 25, 1844, Joseph and Hyrum were wrongfully arrested on charges of treason and delivered to Carthage Jail. Treason is one of the only crimes where those charged can never get bail. This was intentional, to ensure Joseph and Hyrum would be stuck in Carthage Jail for a while.

831. The jail keepers at Carthage Jail were actually very kind to the Mormon prisoners. They fed them good food and even let them use the master bedroom for more protection against the mob.

832. Joseph and Hyrum were prisoners in Carthage Jail, but they did have four friends who stayed with them voluntarily. They were Willard Richards, John Taylor, Stephen Markham, and Dan Jones.

> FOUR OF JOSEPH AND HYRUM'S FRIENDS VOLUNTARILY STAYED WITH THEM IN THE JAIL TO KEEP THEM COMPANY.

833. John Taylor eventually became the third President of The Church of Jesus Christ of Latter-day Saints.

834. On June 26, 1844, the night before the martyrdom, the five men had a peaceful and spiritual meeting. Dan Jones wrote that even some of the guards listened in on the conversation and participated.

835. Understanding the architecture and design of the Carthage Jail building is essential to understanding the story of Joseph and Hyrum's murders. The dining room and living room were downstairs. A staircase lined the back wall. The first door at the top of the stairs led to the jail cell. Joseph and Hyrum were kept there in the days before the martyrdom. After going up the stairs and walking to the left, the next door was the door to the jailor's bedroom. This is where Joseph, Hyrum, Willard Richards, and John Taylor were when the mob arrived and killed Joseph and Hyrum.

836. At almost midnight on June 26, 1844, a mob rushed inside the jail and up the stairs to try to kill the prisoners. The prisoners stood on the other side of the door in calm anticipation, but the mob hesitated. Joseph Smith said boldly, "Come on ye assassins we are ready for you, and would as willingly die now as at daylight." The voice of the Prophet scared the mob away, at least for the time being ("The Martyrdom of Joseph and Hyrum Smith," Dan Jones to Thomas Bolluck).

837. Governor Ford disbanded most of the militia responsible for guarding Carthage Jail and protecting the prisoners. He left eight men to guard the jail. Unfortunately, these men were cooperating with the mob. Governor Ford brought the rest of the militia with him to Nauvoo.

838. Joseph met with his attorney for the last time a few hours before he was killed. His lawyer's name was James H. Woods. Joseph mentioned to him that he would be murdered by the end of the day. After that turned out to be true, Woods said that Joseph proved to him in that moment that he was truly a prophet.

839. The last letter Joseph Smith ever wrote was to his wife Emma. He dictated the letter to Willard Richards, who wrote the letter for him. The very last paragraph, however, was written and signed in the Prophet's own handwriting. He expressed his love for his wife and children. He also expressed his innocence.

JOSEPH'S LAST LETTER WAS WRITTEN TO EMMA, ONLY NINE HOURS BEFORE HE DIED.

840. The letter was written nine hours before Joseph died, at around eight in the morning.

841. Stephen Markham, who was one of Joseph's bodyguards, left the jail to run an errand for Joseph. When he returned, the mob would not allow him back inside. They held him at gunpoint, demanding he get back on his horse.

842. The mob forcefully escorted Markham back to Nauvoo. They stabbed through his shoes with their bayonets, making his feet and ankles very bloody. When he arrived in Nauvoo, the mob threatened his life should he return to Carthage.

843. John Taylor had a beautiful singing voice. Hyrum asked John Taylor to sing all seven verses of a song that was very popular in Nauvoo at the time. It was called "A Poor Wayfaring Man of Grief." It is believed to

have been Joseph Smith's favorite hymn. It is hymn number 29 in LDS hymnbooks today.

844. After John Taylor finished singing the entire song, Joseph asked him to sing it one more time. John did so.

845. "A Poor Wayfaring Man of Grief" is a song about the Savior Jesus Christ. In the sixth verse, the song refers to Christ about to meet "a traitor's doom" in a prison from "lying tongues," similar to what happened to Joseph Smith ("A Poor Wayfaring Man of Grief," LDS Hymnbook).

846. The last two lines of the final verse of "A Poor Wayfaring Man of Grief" are the words of Jesus Christ to a faithful servant, saying, "These deeds shall they memorial be; Fear not, thou didst them unto me" ("A Poor Wayfaring Man of Grief," LDS Hymnbook). Historians believe this line is what prompted Joseph to ask John to sing the song again, knowing the work he did for Christ's Church would cost him his own life, but he found comfort in the final line.

847. During this peaceful spiritual meeting, Hyrum read a passage in the Book of Mormon with the others. He turned down the corner leaf to save the page. It was Ether 12:36–38.

848. Ether 12:36–38 states, "And it came to pass that I prayed unto the Lord that he would give unto the Gentiles grace, that they might have charity. And it came to pass that the Lord said unto me: If they have not charity it mattereth not unto thee, thou hast seen thy weakness, thou shalt be made strong, even unto the sitting down in the place which I have prepared in the mansions of my Father. And now I . . . bid farewell unto the Gentiles; yea, and also unto my brethren whom I love, until we shall meet before the judgement seat of Christ, where all men shall know that my garments are spotted with your blood" (Ether 12:36–38).

849. Around five o' clock in the evening, a mob of about 150–200 armed men with their faces painted black, red, and yellow stormed Carthage Jail.

850. At this point, there were only four men at Carthage Jail. They were Joseph Smith, Hyrum Smith, John Taylor, and Willard Richards.

851. They raced up the stairs. One man led the mob up the stairs, and Joseph Smith punched him in the face. The hit was so powerful that the man rolled all the way back down the stairs.

852. At first, the mob shot into the jail cell, where they thought the prisoners were. The prisoners were not in the jail cell; they were in the jailor's bedroom. This gave the prisoners time to shut the bedroom door and attempt to barricade it before the mob realized they were hiding in there.

853. Stephen Markham left behind a hickory cane (walking stick), which John Taylor used to aim guns away from himself and the others when the mob attacked.

854. John Taylor was shot with four bullets, but he survived with the help of Willard Richards.

855. John Taylor was first shot while running toward the back window, trying to escape.

856. Hyrum was the first of the Smith brothers to be shot.

857. Hyrum was shot to the left of his nose. It was the fatal shot.

858. As Hyrum fell backwards from being shot, he exclaimed, "I'm a dead man!" (Doctrine and Covenants 135:1).

859. Joseph was devastated to see his older brother shot. Joseph sobbed and cried out for his brother.

860. Joseph Smith brought two pistols to Carthage Jail. According to one of his letters to Emma, he normally would not have done so if it weren't for his desire to protect Hyrum and his friends who visited him there. He did not necessarily bring them for his own protection.

861. Once Hyrum was shot, Joseph put his gun down and ran to the window. He jumped out the window and was shot to death in the process.

862. Right when Joseph was climbing out of the window, he was shot twice. He was shot in the leg and also through his chest.

863. As Joseph jumped from the window, his last words were, "Oh Lord! My God!" (Doctrine and Covenants 135:1).

864. As Joseph Smith's body landed on the ground outside, one of the mob members yelled that Joseph jumped through the window. The mob ran outside to go see his body and make sure he was dead.

JOSEPH SMITH'S LAST WORDS WERE "OH LORD! MY GOD!"

865. Then somebody among the mob yelled that an angry crowd of Mormons was coming to attack

them. The mob fled for fear of vengeance, even though there were no Mormon mobs coming to seek revenge at that time. Luckily, though, this meant that Joseph and Hyrum's bodies were left alone without being stolen or brutally mutilated after their deaths. It also meant the lives of John Taylor and Willard Richards were spared.

866. Some think that Joseph possibly fell out of the window on accident when he was shot. In reality, according to Willard Richards and John Taylor, he deliberately jumped.

867. Since he died immediately afterward, there is no way to know whether the Prophet jumped out the window in an attempt to save his own life or to sacrifice his own life to save John Taylor and Willard Richards. It is possible that Joseph knew that since the mob wanted to kill him, if he jumped out the window, he could save his friends. That is what Willard Richards, who witnessed Joseph's death, believed was Joseph's motive. If this is true, he succeeded in saving John Taylor and Willard Richards.

868. Joseph leaped from the second-floor window of Carthage Jail and landed on his left side. Willard Richards looked outside the window to see if he survived. He wrote that he was relieved to see that the Prophet had passed away and was now at rest.

869. Both Joseph and Hyrum Smith were both shot brutally even after they were dead. They both received four fatal bullets.

870. Joseph Smith died at age thirty-eight. Hyrum died at age forty-four.

871. Joseph Smith died as the Prophet and President of The Church of Jesus Christ of Latter-day Saints. Hyrum Smith was the Patriarch of the Church at his death.

872. The mob attack at Carthage Jail was relatively quick. The mob was at Carthage Jail for about ten minutes before they fled the scene.

873. Willard Richards was not injured or shot at all, despite being the biggest of the four men.

874. Joseph once prophesied to Willard Richards that he would one day stand in a hail storm of bullets and not be harmed. Even though Willard Richards did not initially believe it could ever be possible, this prophecy was fulfilled in Carthage Jail.

875. Joseph and Hyrum's younger brother Samuel Harrison Smith tried coming to visit them in Carthage Jail. He was not initially allowed into the city of Carthage until after the murders.

876. When Samuel did finally arrive at the jail, the mob had just killed his brothers. They chased Samuel out of town.

877. Orrin Porter Rockwell, one of Joseph's personal bodyguards, really wanted to go to Carthage with Joseph and Hyrum to try protecting them. He had saved Joseph's life several times before. Joseph told him to stay home.

878. Porter Rockwell decided to go to Carthage to visit his friends anyway. While riding his horse to Carthage, he saw a fellow member of the Church speeding past him toward Nauvoo and being chased by the mob. The man told Porter that the mob killed Joseph and Hyrum. Porter was furious. When the mob reached Porter Rockwell, he stopped, pulled out his rifle, and killed two mob men in only two shots. The horrified mob retreated.

879. Orrin Porter Rockwell often saved Joseph's life, even if it required violence and even killing other people. He is one of the most controversial people in all of LDS Church history. Once Porter passed away, his wife was really worried about his salvation with all his violent actions. She received a patriarchal blessing in which it was revealed that the Lord forgave Porter for all his sins because of how often he saved the Prophet Joseph Smith.

880. Joseph prophesied to Porter that as long as Porter never cut his hair, his enemies would never be able to take his life by bullet. Toward the end of his life, he lived in Utah with many of the Saints. The widow of Don Carlos Smith, younger brother of Joseph, lost all of her hair from typhoid fever in the mid-1850s. Porter cut his hair and gave it to her to use as a wig. Orrin Porter Rockwell died in 1878 of a heart attack.

881. The night of Joseph and Hyrum's murder, Porter rode through the streets of Nauvoo, agonizingly announcing the deaths Joseph and Hyrum.

882. That same day, at around the same time that Joseph and Hyrum were murdered, Emma Smith was serving dinner to Governor Thomas Ford and about sixty militiamen in the Mansion Home. Emma

JOSEPH AND HYRUM'S FUNERALS WERE ON JUNE 29, 1844, THE DAY THAT THEIR TRIAL WAS SUPPOSED TO BE HELD.

did not learn about her husband's death until five hours later, at around 10:00 p.m.

883.   When her sons were killed, Lucy Mack Smith was living with Emma in the Mansion Home.

884.   Joseph and Hyrum's trial was scheduled for June 29, 1844, but they were murdered two days prior. Instead, their funerals were held that day.

AFTER THE MARTYRDOM

885.   The account from John Taylor about the martyrdoms can be found in Doctrine and Covenants 135.

886.   John Taylor wrote after the martyrdom, "Joseph Smith, the Prophet and Seer of the Lord has done more, save Jesus only, for the salvation of men in this world, than any other man that ever lived in it" (Doctrine and Covenants 135:3).

887.   John Taylor continued by saying, "In the short space of twenty years, he has brought forth the Book of Mormon, which he translated by the gift and power of God, and has been the means of publishing it on two continents; has sent the fulness of the gospel, which it contained, to the four quarters of the earth; has brought the revelations and commandments which compose this book of Doctrine and Covenants, and many other wise documents and instructions for the benefit of the children of men; gathered many thousands of the Latter-day Saints, founded a great city, and left a fame and a name that cannot be slain. He lived great, and he died great, in the eyes of God and his people; and like most of the Lord's anointed in ancient times, has sealed his mission and his works with his own blood . . ." (Doctrine and Covenants 135:3).

888.   The night of the Prophet's death, all of nature seemed upset. Dogs barked and cows screamed all night.

889.   Nauvoo was noticeably gloomy and sad in the days following Joseph and Hyrum's deaths. It was even noticed by those passing through the town.

DOGS BARKED AND COWS SCREAMED ALL NIGHT AFTER THE MARTYRDOM.

890. Governor Thomas Ford arranged for Joseph and Hyrum's bodies to be brought back to Nauvoo on the following day, June 28, 1844.

891. Governor Thomas Ford also warned many of the non-Mormons in Illinois to escape from the state for their lives, as the Saints would surely seek revenge. He was wrong; the Saints were commanded by Church leaders not to seek revenge after the martyrdoms.

892. Joseph and Hyrum were carried from Carthage to Nauvoo by two horse-drawn hearses. Willard Richards drove the first hearse. Samuel Harrison Smith drove the second.

893. As the wagons reached Nauvoo, the entire city was outside trying to catch a glimpse of the bodies, likely to try to confirm what they genuinely could not believe to ever be possible. There were thousands of people gathered in the streets of Nauvoo. People even stood on rooftops to try to get a better look.

894. Many of the Saints had wanted to avenge the deaths of Joseph and Hyrum. However, Church leaders still in Nauvoo told the Saints to do nothing until the complete Quorum of the Twelve returned to Nauvoo.

895. Luckily, four days before the Prophet's death, he wrote letters to the Twelve telling them to return to Nauvoo immediately. They all arrived relatively soon after Joseph's death. The Twelve ordered that the Saints remain peaceful and let the law handle it—and when that failed, to let God handle it.

896. The bodies were delivered to the Mansion Home in Nauvoo. The only people allowed to be inside to see the bodies at that time were members of the Smith family. All others would have to wait until the memorial services the next day.

897. After the bodies were washed and dressed in burial clothes, they were brought into the main room of the Mansion Home for the family to see and get closure.

898. Emma Smith was so distraught that she fainted at the sight of her dead husband. She had to be carried out of the room.

899. When Lucy Mack Smith saw the bodies of her two sons, along with the pain and sorrow of the rest of her family, she cried in agony to God, "My God, my God, why hast thou forsaken this family?" A voice replied, "I have taken them to myself, that they might have rest" (Lucy Mack Smith, *The History of Joseph Smith by His Mother*, 286).

900. Newel Knight, who was one of the earliest members of the Church, wrote in his journal after the deaths of Joseph and Hyrum Smith. He wrote that if it were not for his wife and children, he would feel as though he had nothing else to live for. He loved Joseph and Hyrum so much. He vowed to himself that he would live worthy enough to be with Joseph and Hyrum again after his own death.

901. William W. Phelps was a great writer. Joseph Smith loved his use of words, which is why William W. Phelps was scribe, editor, songwriter, and creator of multiple Church newspapers. The song "Praise to the Man" was written by William W. Phelps about Joseph Smith after the Prophet's death. The song was written to the tune of a Scottish folk song, which is why the tune is often played with bagpipes in movies.

902. When Joseph and Hyrum Smith passed away, photography was in its infancy. When somebody died back then, death masks were created on the deceased person's face from clay. It was how they preserved what the person looked like. The death masks made of Joseph and Hyrum Smith in the hours following their deaths are now used to help sculptors and painters portray the Prophet and his brother as accurately as possible.

903. Two coffins, which most believed contained the bodies of Joseph and Hyrum at the time, were buried in the public graveyard. However, these coffins were actually filled with sand.

JOSEPH AND HYRUM'S PUBLIC COFFINS HELD NOTHING BUT SAND. THE REAL COFFINS WERE SECRETLY BURIED UNDER THE NAUVOO HOUSE.

904. Emma Smith had Joseph and Hyrum's real coffins secretly buried underneath the Nauvoo House so they would be safe from the mob and grave diggers.

905. Their bodies were secretly moved several times to different locations to ensure that they would remain safe from evil men. Years and years later, once it was deemed safe, Joseph, Hyrum, and Emma received official, marked graves in Nauvoo, Illinois.

906. The mob men responsible for Joseph and Hyrum's murder were sent to trial for their crimes. However, they were all acquitted at the trial for Joseph's murder. The prosecutors never showed up for the trial of Hyrum's murder, so the judge dismissed the defendants. Nobody, besides

those two men killed by Porter Rockwell, was ever held responsible for the murders of Joseph and Hyrum in their mortal life.

SUCCESSION CONFUSION

907.   After Joseph and Hyrum's deaths, the question arose among the Saints: "Who will lead the Church now?"

908.   Sidney Rigdon, the only remaining member of the First Presidency of the Church, organized a meeting before the Twelve were supposed to return.

909.   Brigham Young, President of the Quorum of the Twelve, arrived the night before the meeting and was therefore able to attend. At the time, Brigham Young was generally considered by most of the Saints as the unofficial leader of the Church.

910.   The meeting was held on August 8, 1844.

911.   Almost the entire Church was in attendance at the meeting.

912.   At the meeting, Sidney Rigdon spoke for about two hours. He claimed that he saw a vision. The Lord wanted him to be the guardian of the Church for the time being.

913.   The Saints who wrote about this meeting said that Sidney's speech seemed very out of character for him. He was normally an eloquent speaker, but this time he seemed unorganized and strange. The Saints wrote that it seemed like there was no inspiration or spirit behind his speech, even if his intentions were pure.

914.   After Sidney Rigdon was done speaking, Brigham Young stood up to speak. He stated that if the Saints desired to have Sidney Rigdon to lead the Church, then he could lead the Church. He said that the Twelve, however, had the keys of the kingdom bestowed upon them by Joseph Smith.

915.   While Brigham Young spoke, his face, countenance, voice, and gestures began to exactly resemble the Prophet Joseph Smith. Anson Call, among many other Saints, wrote about Brigham Young's speech at this meeting. He wrote that when Brigham Young spoke, his voice began to sound just like Joseph's. Call said that if he were not looking directly at Brigham Young as he spoke, he would have thought Joseph Smith was

speaking. Anson Call said he knew the Spirit was telling him to follow Brigham Young and the Quorum of the Twelve.

916. After both Brigham Young and Sidney Rigdon spoke, they held a vote among all in attendance. When they asked for those who desired to be led by Sidney Rigdon, not a single person voted in favor. When it was asked who desired to be led by Brigham Young and the Quorum of the Twelve Apostles, every person voted in the affirmative. The decision was made.

917. Sidney Rigdon became bitter and eventually started his own church based on the teachings of Joseph Smith and the Book of Mormon. He had a small following, but the church he founded has since gone extinct.

THE NAUVOO EXODUS

918. Even though the founder of The Church of Jesus Christ of Latter-day Saints was gone, the Church was still strong and flourishing.

919. The tension and mob violence against the Saints continued to increase. Brigham Young realized that Nauvoo was no longer safe for the Saints to reside.

920. Shortly after the Nauvoo Temple was finished and dedicated, Brigham Young led the first company of Saints to the Rocky Mountains.

921. Brigham Young began leading the Saints to the western United States in February 1846.

922. They left in three groups. The first group left with Brigham Young in February. The first group of Saints consisted of about 2,500 people.

923. The second company of Saints was the largest group. There were approximately 12,000 saints. They left in April 1846.

924. The final group left in the fall of 1846. It was the smallest group. They suffered a lot during their winter expedition.

925. The Mormon pioneers traveling west experienced many trials and sorrows. Many men, women, and children starved or froze to death. Family members and friends were often buried along the journey.

926. Brigham Young beheld a vision of God's destination for the Saints. He knew exactly what it looked like before they arrived.

927. After a long journey, Brigham Young became extremely sick. He rode in a wagon. Finally, Brigham Young peeked outside of his wagon and recognized the location from his vision. He knew they had finally reached their destination. He told the company to stop and set up camp.

928. It was in this general location that the Church's headquarters was established, where the next temple began construction, and where thousands of Saints found a permanent home. This place is now known as Salt Lake City, Utah.

EMMA SMITH AFTER THE MARTYRDOM

929. Emma Smith decided to stay in Illinois to raise her family instead of moving west. She never lost her faith in the Church or the work; she just wished to live the rest of her life in peace with her children after all she had gone through.

930. Joseph and Emma had eleven children together. Only five of those children lived to adulthood.

> OF JOSEPH AND EMMA'S ELEVEN CHILDREN, ONLY FIVE LIVED TO ADULTHOOD.

931. Joseph and Emma's children were: Alvin (June 15, 1828–June 15, 1828), twins Thaddeus and Louisa (April 30, 1831–April 30, 1831), Joseph Murdock Smith (April 30, 1831–March 29, 1832), Julia Murdock Smith (April 30, 1831–September 12, 1880), Joseph III (November 6, 1832–December 10, 1914), Frederick (June 20, 1836–April 13, 1862), Alexander (June 2, 1838–August 12, 1909), Don Carlos (June 13, 1840–September 15, 1841), an unnamed male child who was stillborn (February 6, 1842–February 6, 1842), and David Hyrum (November 17, 1844–August 29, 1904).

932. Emma only gave birth in her own home once. It was the birth of David Hyrum in 1844, months after Joseph Smith's death.

933. After the Battle of Nauvoo, Emma moved to Fulton, Illinois, for the safety of her family. She moved there with a few friends.

934. An old friend of hers, Thomas Bernhisel, wrote a letter to her with bad news. He told her that the man leasing the Mansion Home from her was actually stealing her furniture. She returned to Nauvoo immediately and caught the thief in the act. She was able to stop him.

935. She moved back into the Mansion Home in Nauvoo. One of the men who helped her become manager of the Mansion Home again (basically impossible for women at that time to own property by themselves) was Lewis C. Bidamon.

936. Lewis C. Bidamon was a non-Mormon, but he admired Joseph Smith. He was a heavy drinker and was married and divorced two times before. He had two daughters from two different women, one of which was illegitimate.

937. Lewis C. Bidamon helped provide for Emma. It was his kindness and assistance that made her decide to marry him. He was sweet to her and was a good stepfather to her children.

938. Emma Smith and Lewis C. Bidamon were married on December 23, 1847.

939. If the date of their marriage sounds familiar, it was actually the Prophet Joseph Smith's birthday. As insensitive as that sounds, Emma and Lewis were married on that date because it was the only day that the minister who could perform the ceremony was in town.

940. The Mormon settlers in Utah were appalled and angry with Emma for marrying Lewis Bidamon. Not only did she marry a new man on Joseph Smith's birthday, but he was a non-Mormon with a horrible reputation in the community.

941. While Emma initially supported Brigham Young and the Twelve, she heard rumors that Brigham was saying extremely insulting things about her out west. She started saying vicious things about him. They began to hate each other. They were thousands of miles away, which made actual communication more difficult. The rumor mill likely aggravated and exaggerated the drama and tension between them.

942. Emma was sealed to Joseph for eternity before his death, but she was never sealed to Lewis. Lewis was always very supportive and respectful of her relationship to Joseph Smith.

943. In 1860, the Saints who had stayed back in Nauvoo decided to re-form the Church that they were once a part of before the bulk of the members moved west. They asked Joseph Smith III to become their leader,

President, and Prophet. At first, he refused. Eventually he reluctantly consented. Emma was hesitant about this as well but was ultimately supportive. They called their church The Re-Organized Church of Jesus Christ of Latter-day Saints. It has since been renamed the Community of Christ.

944. After seventeen years of marriage, Lewis Bidamon had an affair with a younger woman named Nancy Abercrombie. He got her pregnant. Months later, Nancy gave birth to a healthy boy named Charles.

> EMMA SMITH RAISED FOUR CHILDREN THAT WERE NOT HER OWN.

945. When Charles reached the age of about four years old, Nancy was no longer financially able to care for him. She brought him to Emma. Emma raised Charles until her death like one of her own children.

946. Charles was one of four children that Emma raised that were not biologically her own. She and Joseph adopted twins in Kirtland, a boy and a girl. The boy passed away at only a few months old, but the girl, Julia, lived to adulthood.

947. The fourth child that Emma raised who was not her own was Elizabeth Agnes Kendall. Her mother, widow Elizabeth Kendall, was a good friend of Emma's before she died when she gave birth to her daughter, Elizabeth. Elizabeth Agnes Kendall was left with her stepfather and, eventually, her new stepmother. When she was eight years old, they realized they could not financially care for her anymore.

948. Elizabeth Agnes Kendall ended up in the care of Emma. Emma raised her like one of her own. Elizabeth eventually married Emma's biological son, Alexander Hale Smith.

949. What happened to Charles's mother, Nancy Abercrombie? Emma hired her to work as a housemaid in their home so she could always be close to her son.

950. Emma and Lewis were married for almost thirty-two years at her death in 1879. That is more than twice as long as she was married to Joseph Smith.

951. Emma Hale Smith Bidamon died on April 30, 1879, at the age of seventy-five in the Nauvoo House.

952. She died on the anniversary of the death of her biological twins whom she lost in Kirtland.

953. On her deathbed, Emma asked her husband Lewis to promise to marry Nancy Abercrombie. He kept his promise and married Nancy shortly after.

954. Emma's last words were said in a sweet whisper, "Joseph ... Joseph ... Joseph." Then she stretched out her left hand and said, "Joseph! Yes, yes, I'm coming."

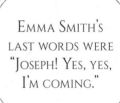

EMMA SMITH'S LAST WORDS WERE "JOSEPH! YES, YES, I'M COMING."

SMITH FAMILY AFTER THE MARTYRDOMS

955. Lucy Mack Smith desired to go west with the rest of the Saints. It is believed that Emma wanted her to stay so she could take care of Lucy.

956. Sophronia, Joseph's older sister, was supposed to go west with the Saints. Her husband went ahead first, but never returned. Historians believe that he died when he reached Winter Quarters in Nebraska. When her husband did not return, Sophronia decided to stay with her mother and sister-in-law in Nauvoo.

957. After being chased by the mob and with the stress of losing his older brothers, Samuel Harrison Smith suffered many health complications in the weeks after the martyrdoms. He died a little over a month later on July 30, 1844, of a fever caused by overexertion. The Smith family had lost three sons/brothers/husbands in about one month.

958. Joseph's younger brother William was initially a huge supporter of Brigham Young and the Quorum of the Twelve Apostles. However, he soon turned against them and became an influential leader in the reformed Latter-day Saint church, now called the Community of Christ.

959. Katherine Smith Salisbury, Joseph's younger sister, settled and stayed in Hancock County, Illinois, for the rest of her life. Her children and family often suffered through persecution because they were related to the Prophet Joseph Smith. They were even threatened and shot at several times.

960. In the 1850s, several Utah Saints came back to Illinois to visit Lucy and Emma Smith frequently.

961. Lucy Mack Smith was the Church's first biographer. With a little help from Martha and Howard Coray, she wrote an autobiography called *The History of Lucy Mack Smith by Herself* in late 1844. The title was changed years later to *The History of Joseph Smith by His Mother*.

962. Lucy Mack Smith did not die alone. She was with family. Lucy lived with Emma at the time. Her grandson Joseph Smith III was there holding her hand next to her bed until she died.

963. Lucy once said that if she did move west, when she died she wanted her body sent back to Nauvoo so she could be buried with her family. She never moved west though. When she died, she was buried next to Joseph Smith Sr. in Nauvoo.

Joseph Smith's Personality

964. Joseph was very insecure about his writing skills, since he was not very educated. This is why he often employed scribes and why he had so much anxiety when the commandment to document the history of the Church was revealed to him.

965. The Prophet had an innate happy disposition. He was a positive and cheerful man, regardless of his worst trials.

966. Joseph Smith loved deeply and had profound compassion for other people.

967. One night, Joseph answered a knock at the door of the Mansion Home in Nauvoo. It was two African American women who had escaped slavery. They told the Prophet they had no place to go. Joseph called Emma downstairs and they decided that the women would stay in their home. One of the women stayed even until after the Prophet's death. For the first time in their lives, they were treated as equal members of the family, not slaves or servants.

968. Regardless of his love and compassion, he could scold and rebuke those same people he loved very sharply.

969. Joseph Smith was humble and honest about who he truly was in the eyes of God. He was asked several times if he was Jesus Christ or God. He always answered in the negative, saying he was only a man who was called to serve God.

970. John Taylor once said that even though Joseph Smith was uneducated and ignorant in the academic sense, he was one of the most intelligent men John had ever met, because Joseph was taught by God and angels.

971. Joseph Smith loved to have fun and be silly. He could even be a bit of a prankster. Because he was so joyful and fun-loving, many people left the Church, believing that a real prophet of God would not act in such a

way. Many believed that Hyrum Smith—more solemn and serious than his brother—seemed to have the personality of a prophet.

972. He loved playing games with the kids and young men. They would sometimes draw a line in the sand and jump as far as they could in front of it and then challenge others to try beating their distance. They loved wrestling too. They also would hold a wooden stick in between two people, sit on the ground with both feet touching the other person's, then pull the stick. The weaker of the two competitors would be forced to stand up. Joseph and his friends played several other games as well.

973. Joseph was a large, physically strong man. Since he was not very educated and not necessarily good with words, he sometimes solved problems by getting into physical fights with other men. It is believed that this is one of those things he constantly felt the need to repent for.

974. Once when Joseph Smith was Mayor of Nauvoo, a fight broke out in the street. He immediately broke up the fight and jokingly said that he, Joseph, was the only person allowed to fight in Nauvoo.

> JOSEPH WAS NOT NECESSARILY GOOD WITH WORDS AND WOULD SOMETIMES SOLVE PROBLEMS BY GETTING INTO PHYSICAL FIGHTS WITH OTHER MEN.

975. On April 12, 1834, Joseph wrote in his journal about spending the entire day fishing with the brethren. The next day, he was too sick from the day before to attend Church.

976. Joseph Smith was not a perfect person. He frequently and often had to pray for forgiveness of his sins.

977. Joseph Smith had an innocent and pure countenance. When Eliza R. Snow met Joseph Smith for the first time, Joseph was visiting with her father in the Snows' home. She secretly observed him while he warmed his hands by the fireplace. She studied his face. She determined, based on this experience, that he was an honest man.

978. While Joseph Smith was generally confident in his strengths and prophetic abilities, he was not prideful.

979. Joseph, of course, did not enjoy trials. Regardless, he was willing to endure and learn from his trials, especially after his experience in Liberty Jail.

980. The Prophet was a pristine, neat, and organized man. He kept a clean desk and office.

981. Contrary to what most might assume, Joseph did not often speak about his most sacred spiritual experiences. For example, most of the Saints were not aware of his First Vision experience until after his death, because it was so sacred and special. It also was a huge source of persecution when he spoke about it.

982. Joseph Smith was an emotional man. He was not afraid to show his emotions or cry in front of people. The tears flowed from eyes often and easily.

983. Joseph would sometimes dress in awful and worn-out clothing to go meet those docking in Nauvoo. He would ask them why they came. If they said they had come because they joined the Church, then he would ask what they thought of Joseph Smith. As new converts, their answer was always positive. Then he would tell them that he himself is Joseph Smith. He would do this in awful clothing in an attempt to try to show people that he was a normal human being. He did not want members to expect perfection from him.

984. Joseph Smith once said about himself, "Although I do wrong, I do not the wrongs I am charged with doing; the wrong that I do is through the frailty of human nature, like other men. No man lives without fault" (Joseph Smith, in *History of the Church*, 5:140).

985. During the construction of the Kirtland Temple, Joseph was under a lot of pressure and stress with that, along with other responsibilities like the bank and steam mill too. One day, he was being bombarded with questions. He became frustrated and stormed off. A man followed him and asked for his help for a few minutes. Joseph responded with a very rude, condescending reply. The man who asked for his help must have been hurt by the Prophet's rude remark. Joseph Smith was not perfect. He, like everyone else, had the capacity to let frustration allow him to say things that offend others.

986. Those who met the Prophet Joseph Smith in his lifetime either loved him or hated him. Very few who met him ever felt impartial.

987. Joseph loved going on sleigh rides with Emma and their family. It was what they

JOSEPH AND EMMA OFTEN WENT ON SLEIGH RIDES WHILE THEY WERE COURTING.

did on "dates" when they were courting. One winter, they went sleigh riding almost daily.

988. Joseph was very forgiving. He often gave people second or third chances even after they betrayed him.

989. Joseph Smith was very knowledgeable about the scriptures because he was taught by the authors themselves.

990. Especially after his betrayal and loneliness in Liberty Jail, the Prophet taught about loyalty and the importance of friendship, love, and harmony in the Church.

991. Peter H. Burnett, Joseph's attorney while he was in Liberty Jail, once wrote about the Prophet's strong and confident personality that he witnessed in the few days before Joseph was incarcerated. He said that in only five days, Joseph was able to soften his captors and he could be around them without harm or danger.

992. Joseph Smith has been described as having bad manners and being rough around the edges.

993. Joseph's sermons were very rarely documented because most of the Saints felt like his sermons were better when he was speaking by revelation. Otherwise, it was easy to tell that the Prophet was not very educated. They did not think his regular sermons were important enough to document. Joseph was not weak in speaking, though, just uneducated.

994. Joseph Smith learned and taught gospel principles little by little. It is how the Lord wants us to learn: line upon line, precept upon precept.

Miscellaneous

995. Joseph Smith had a white mastiff dog for many years before his death. The dog's name was Major. He had a bulldog named Baker at one point too. He and Emma also owned a few horses.

996. Joseph Smith had more than 250 legal encounters during his lifetime.

997. The Prophet was a little over six feet two inches tall. He weighed over 200 pounds, and therefore was very strong physically.

998. Joseph had thick, straight, dark blonde (or light brown) hair. It was receding a little bit by the time he died, partially from being poisoned and partially from stress.

> JOSEPH HAD A WHITE MASTIFF NAMED MAJOR AND A BULLDOG NAMED BAKER.

999. He had deep hazel and blue eyes and a light complexion.

1000. Joseph had an oval-shaped face with a large nose. He had a long upper lip, thick eyebrows, and long eyelashes.

1001. Joseph Smith was described by many people as good looking and handsome.

BIBLIOGRAPHY

The Church of Jesus Christ of Latter-day Saints, www.lds.org.

"Church History." *Church History,* history.lds.org.

"Joseph Smith Papers," BYUtv, www.byutv.org/show/5d739281-537f-40f3-92ed-8a60b9f25fb0.

The Church Historian's Press. *The Joseph Smith Papers: A comprehensive digital collection of the papers of Joseph Smith,* www.josephsmithpapers.org. Accessed 18 Sept. 2017.

The Doctrine and Covenants. Independence, MO, Joseph Smith Jr.'s Rare Reprints, 1990.

Smith, Joseph, and Joseph Fielding Smith. *Teachings of the Prophet Joseph Smith.* American Fork, UT: Covenant Communications Inc., 2002.

Smith, Joseph, and Dean C. Jessee. *The Joseph Smith Papers.* Salt Lake City: The Church Historian's Press, 2008.

Smith, Lucy, and Preston Nibley. *History of Joseph Smith.* Whitefish, MT: Kessinger Pub., 2005.

The Book of Mormon. Palmyra, NY, The Church of Jesus Christ of Latter-day Saints, 1830.

The Book of Mormon: Another Testament of Jesus Christ, The Doctrine and Covenants of The Church of Jesus Christ of Latter-day Saints, The Pearl of Great Price. Salt Lake City, UT: The Church of Jesus Christ of Latter-day Saints, 1999.

Elders' Journal of The Church of Jesus Christ of Latter-day Saints. Far West, MO, 1837–1838.

Latter Day Saints' Messenger and Advocate. Kirtland, Ohio, Oct. 1834–Sept. 1837.

"Letter from David R. Atchison, Boonville, MO, to Lilburn W. Boggs," 5 Oct. 1838, in "Document Containing the Correspondence," 35.

Nauvoo Neighbor. Nauvoo, IL: The Church of Jesus Christ of Latter-day Saints, 1843.

"Missouri Execution Order 44," "Mormon War Papers, MSA." Lilburn W. Boggs, Jefferson City, MO, to John B. Clark, 27 Oct. 1838.

Pratt, Parley P. *The Autobiography of Parley Parker Pratt.* United States: Deseret Book, 2000.

Original Manuscript of the Book of Mormon, The Church of Jesus Christ of Latter-day Saints, 1830.

Original Manuscript of *Joseph Smith's Translation of the Bible,* Community of Christ.

Richards, Willard. "Journal Excerpt, 23–27 June 1844," *The Joseph Smith Papers,* 37.

Call, Anson. Personal Journal, 1854.

Autobiography (1800–1846), "Newel Knight's Journal," *Classic Experiences and Adventures.* Salt Lake City: Bookcraft, 1969.

Stevenson, Edward. *Reminiscences of Joseph the Prophet, and the Coming Forth of the Book of Mormon,* 1893.

Thompson, Mercy F. "Recollections of the Prophet Joseph Smith." *Juvenile Instructor* 27, no. 13 (1 July 1892), 398.

Thompson, Mercy F. "Letter to My Posterity," cited in Pearson H. Corbett, *Hyrum Smith, Patriarch,* 1963, 201.

Taylor, John. "The Martyrdom of Joseph Smith," 1844.

Pratt, Parley P. *Millennial Star.* The Church of Jesus Christ of Latter-day Saints, 1840.

Coray, Howard. *Reminiscences.* Brigham Young Universtiy, ca. 1883.

Smith, George A. "My Journal." *Instructor,* May 1946, 217.

Recollection of Brigham Young, unpublished discourse, July 14, 1861, Church Archives.

Times and Seasons. Nauvoo, IL: The Church of Jesus Christ of Latter-day Saints, 1839–1846.

ABOUT THE AUTHOR

ALEXA EREKSON was born in Nevada, where she has lived her entire life. She has always had a deep connection and love for the Prophet Joseph Smith, so much so that she sometimes wondered if her "obsession" was considered "normal." She never expected to become a writer. She wanted to be a registered nurse. However, the Lord had other plans for her. In early 2016, she became very ill, and the doctors discovered that her stomach is paralyzed. Her condition, idiopathic gastroparesis, is debilitating. She had to drop out of nursing school and quit her job. She became depressed. One day, she decided that with all her knowledge about theme parks, she should write fact books about them. Thus, her first book, *Disney Till You're Dizzy: 1,001 Facts, Rumors, and Myths about the Disneyland Resort*, was born! She now has a blast writing theme park books, regardless of her illnesses and limitations. Writing about the Prophet Joseph Smith, though, has been her favorite. It has been life-changing. She wrote this book to help others understand the life and personality of Joseph Smith Jr., and she hopes that it builds the testimonies of all those who read it.

Scan to visit

www.alexaerekson.com